WOODTURNING

WOODWORKER GUIDE

WOODTURNING

MICHAEL O'DONNELL

ARGUS BOOKS

Argus Books Limited
Wolsey House,
Wolsey Road,
Hemel Hempstead,
Hertfordshire HP2 4SS

First published by Argus Books 1988

© Michael O'Donnell 1988

ISBN 0 85242 901 0

Phototypesetting by En to En, Tunbridge Wells, Kent
Printed and bound by Richard Clay Ltd, Chichester, Sussex

CONTENTS

ACKNOWLEDGEMENTS

Photographer: Joanne B. O'Donnell

Cover picture: Glyn Satterley

Robert Sorby, Sheffield, for the information on tools

INTRODUCTION

"WOODTURNING" is the craft (or possibly art) of making objects on a lathe. This is a very basic definition but one which allows the turner complete freedom of technique, expression, and product.

Woodturning can be anything from a satisfying hobby to big business and mass production. It varies from the turner who produces traditional items to the craftsman who continues to explore the craft and extend its boundaries. One thing all turners have in common is the desire to work in the most efficient and effective manner, using the best tool, shaped and sharpened appropriately and presented to the wood for easy turning. Techniques and tools are developing continuously, and old ideas are constantly being questioned. At the present time there are very few basic rules, more a collection of individual experiences shared in a spirit of camaraderie.

Turning requires a sympathetic, intimate relationship between the craftsman, wood, tools and machinery which can only develop and prosper from a very basic understanding of their properties.

My aim in this book is to look at turning from the most basic practical level, breaking down the process into its basic individual components and examining them separately to provide an understanding of the wood and all the different tools. Then I shall bring all the component parts together in exercises designed to consolidate the theories and show the full potential of the tools in such a way as to lay a firm foundation on which individuals can develop their own skills.

The views and ideas are my own, put together as a 'Woodturning Package Deal' designed to stimulate and educate the turner, at the same time making a small contribution from my experience as a woodturner to the continuing development of woodturning technique.

WOODTURNING FOR EVERYONE

Woodturning means different things to different people. For some it's the excitement of using a piece of equipment and if a product emerges then that is a bonus, to others it is just another necessary process in making a particular object. Most turners probably fit somewhere between these extremes and gain satisfaction from both the process and the product. That is where they begin to differ again, for the range of products that can be made on a lathe is enormous. Items can be functional or decorative, large or small, heavy or light. There are virtually no limits to what can be made except for the capacity of the lathe, which is more a function of space and finance, and the imagination of the turner which can develop considerably with experience and education.

It does not matter what you make as long as it brings you the pleasure or profit that you are looking for. Don't belittle your own area of turning by saying things like 'I *only* make _____.' Be proud of it. You only need to worry about what other people think when you start to give pieces to your relations or try to sell them through craft fairs or local shops.

The one thing all turners should have in common is an open and enquiring mind, always be on the look out for something new. Look at other peoples work, criticise or praise it, pick out the good and bad points and even go home and copy it. But don't just look at wooden objects for inspiration, there is a whole world of ceramics, glass and metal to be explored and even combined with wood.

At the present time in the UK, the development of woodturning is primarily equipment-led, with the turner being bombarded with expensive solutions to problems they have not encountered and in many cases they will never encounter. Be canny how you spend your money because it can be either an expensive or cheap hobby and it all depends on you. I have defined woodturning as a process. I stick by that, but add that it should be a way of thinking — thinking about products, problems, solutions and developments for the future. Whatever happens it isn't going to stand still.

THE CUTTING EDGE

The action of turning a piece of wood on a lathe is a relatively simple operation. Almost anything pushed against the revolving wood will remove shavings or polish the surface in some way and no matter how crude the technique or results, it is 'woodturning'.

Some form of tool will improve both technique and results. A file or even a chain saw are possibilities, not that I would recommend any of them. To start with we should be thinking in terms of standard tools made for the job. (I didn't say designed because many of the tools are not.) Understanding just how the tools remove the waste and leave a good finish is essential because with this information you will know which tool to use for any given situation, how to present the cutting edge to the work, how to shape and sharpen the tool, analyse any problems and even design your own tools for special applications.

First we should know what we want from the tools:

1. To remove the waste in a quick, easy and efficient manner.
2. To produce a good clean finished surface.
3. To give good control in obtaining the final form or shape required.
4. To be as safe as possible in use.

The part of the tool which is going to achieve these functions is that which is in contact with the wood. All the rest of the tool is there to allow us to control just how, where and when that contact is made.

In my opinion there are two basic methods by which turning tools cut and shape the wood:

1. Removing the surface waste which is cut up into shavings and dust as in scraping and peeling.
2. Separating two parts of the wood, usually the finished piece and the waste as we would get from slicing and pointing.

Peeling and Scraping

Peeling

This is much the same action as we would use to peel an apple or

3

Fig. 2.1 Peeling cut. Working towards the centre because that is the way the cutting edge is facing. The line at bevel is tangential just below the cut face

Fig. 2.2

Peeling cut

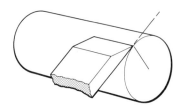

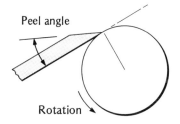

Peel angle

Rotation

orange. Using an acute cutting edge (a knife) and passing it tangentially over the fruit just below the surface, the skin comes off in a long unbroken piece.

Relating this to turning we can see in *(Fig. 2.1)* an acute edged tool is being pushed into the wood with the lower surface (the bevel) tangential to the cut face and peeling off the shavings. With the angle of the tool small, around 30–40°, and the depth of cut fine, the cutting edge severs the shaving from the wood as it moves around. The finer the cutting edge, the less the cutting force and the better the finish.

With the square edge of the tool set parallel to the axis, it can be seen that the only direction in which it can move and still cut the wood, is towards the centre because that is the way the cutting edge is facing. Working along the surface would have to be done in steps.

If the cutting edge were to be swung round about 45° towards the proposed direction of travel, keeping the under surface of the tool (the bevel) tangential to the surface, the cutting edge would face both the rotating wood which will allow it to cut, and also face along the piece which will allow it to travel in that direction.

Fig. 2.3

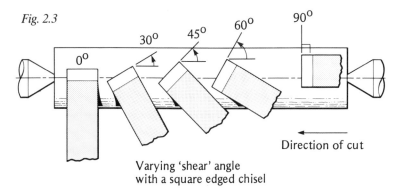

0°   30°   45°   60°   90°

Direction of cut

Varying 'shear' angle
with a square edged chisel

Fig. 2.4 Effect of increasing shear angle on the perceived cutting angle of the tool

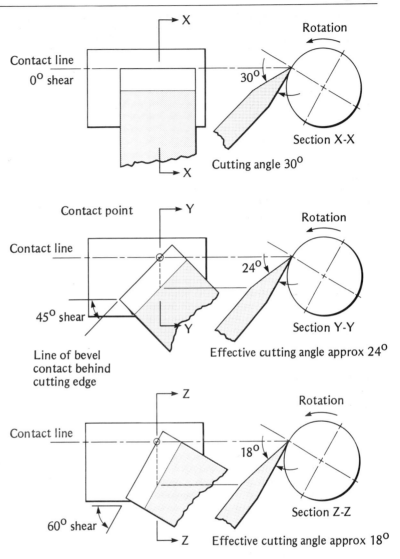

With the cutting edge at around 45°, the type of cut taken is still a 'peeling' cut, but because the cutting edge isn't square to the rotating surface it becomes a 'shear' peeling cut. The amount of shear depends upon exactly how far round the tool is swung from the initial peeling position which has zero shear. This can be quantified in terms of 0% to 100% shear, or a more definite measurement of 0° to 90° of shear. At 90° shear the cutting edge will be at 90° to the axis. The edge is facing the direction of travel but not facing the rotation of the wood, therefore no cutting can take place.

In making this move, two other things have also changed:

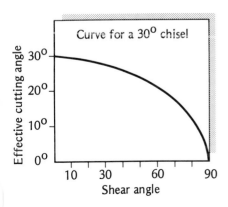

1. The angle of peel presented to the wood by the tool is reduced. At 0° shear, the peel angle is the same as the angle of the tool; at

5

Fig. 2.5 Scraping cut. Tool being pushed straight into the wood towards the centre

Fig. 2.6 Scraping cut. Tool being pushed straight into the wood towards the centre, moving along in steps

Fig. 2.7

90° shear, the angle of peel is theoretically 0° because it is along the cutting edge. In between it will be proportional to the angle of shear. And again as we would find when planing, the finer the angle of peel the better the finished surface obtained.

2. The 'bevel' is now rubbing on the surface of the wood *behind* the cutting edge in the direction of travel. By using this contact surface we can have control over direction of the cutting edge, pivoting *on this surface* to go into or out of the wood or holding steady to produce a flat surface. It also gives stability and support to the tool as it is held firmly against the wood.

The shear peeling cut allows us to work along a surface parallel to the axis only.

Scraping

This is an action where the cutting edge is at 90°, or thereabouts, to the surface. Just as you would use a knife to take a small portion of

Scraping cut

Rotation

Scraper at 90°

Cutting edge at 90° to tangent

Fig. 2.8 Scraping cut. Tool turned round 90 degrees to face along the piece of wood

Fig. 2.9

Scraper movements

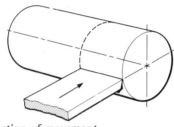

Direction of movement
square edged scraper

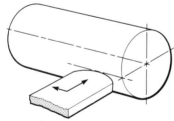

Direction of movement
rounded edged scraper

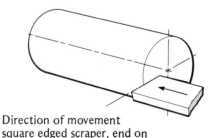

Direction of movement
square edged scraper, end on

butter from the surface of a pack – the butter does not come off in a long peel but gathers in a curled up lump in front of the knife.

Fig. 2.8 Shows a 'clean' edged tool pushed into the wood at right angles to the surface and removing shavings. This action is called 'scraping' and it is somewhat difficult to define the precise nature of the cutting, or possibly pushing, process. This sharp edge will take a very fine shaving. The shaving will hit the top surface of the tool and immediately buckle in order to move on. The cutting force is quite high. Increasing the depth of cut causes the cutting action to break down, resulting in torn grain and increased forces on the tool which pushes the cutting edge down and in most situations draws it further into the wood. It attempts to produce a much thicker and stronger shaving. When this comes into contact with the top of the tool, the shaving will not bend as before. It will be much more like a head-on collision. The force on the tool will be very high, causing it to move downwards until it is clear of the wood, or, if the force is resisted by leverage on the handle, the rotation of the wood can be stopped. Whichever happens, it is usually called a 'dig in'.

The cutting action of the tool is greatly improved by leaving a 'burr' on the edge of the tool, which is a result of grinding. The cutting forces are less and the results are better. If we were to examine the cutting action of the burr microscopically then we would probably find that it is 'peeling' off very fine shavings. Again increasing the depth of cut would produce a much stronger shaving with the same results as before. The big difference is that it would probably happen much more suddenly because there would be a change in cutting method and not just an increase in size of cut.

The square edged tool shown can only cut towards the centre because that is the way it is facing. To enable the scraper to move along the surface it could be swung round to face along the wood. The further it is turned for a given depth of cut, the less the area of contact on the cutting edge.

At 90°, the area of cutting edge is minimal and removal of waste is very fast and efficient with the tool being pushed directly into the waste where the finish is irrelevant. The finished surface is usually rough with limited form control from the side of the tool contacting the wood, but of course this may also cut if sharp. The risk of digging in appears to be minimal.

Alternatively the edge can be ground in a shallow curve so that there is a part of the cutting edge facing the direction of travel while some of the edge faces the finished surface, this can then be pushed or drawn along the surface with a limited depth of cut. The scraper is always around 90° to the rotating wood. It can be used in any direction without altering the presentation of the tool face.

In the extreme situations the difference between peeling and scraping is very apparent, but as the cutting angles come closer together and the burred edge is used, the differences become blurred. As a rough suggestion I would say 0–60° is peeling, 61–90° is scraping, although there is probably some overlap depending on the edge of the tool and the thickness of the shaving.

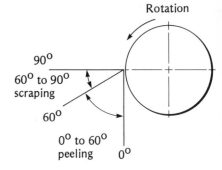

Scraping and peeling cutting angles

Fig. 2.10

Slicing and Pointing

Pointing and slicing are two other methods by which we cut the wood in particular situations. They are similar in that they separate two sections of the wood and do not create any shavings.

Slicing

Slicing is a cutting action where a sharp cutting edge is drawn across the surface being cut. This is not sawing because a saw has many cutting edges, although it can be drawn backwards and forwards moving the blade across the surface until it has cut through. Slicing bread, tomatoes or bacon are probably the situations where we can automatically think of this type of cutting. The material to be cut is relatively soft and would probably crush before being cut if the sharp edge were just pressed down on it. The piece sliced off is not waste and could be of any thickness, because the bread, tomato or bacon yields to allow the whole of the cutting implement to pass through. In these situations it is the cutting edge that is moving, but it is the relative movement of the material and the cutting edge that matters, therefore either could be moving.

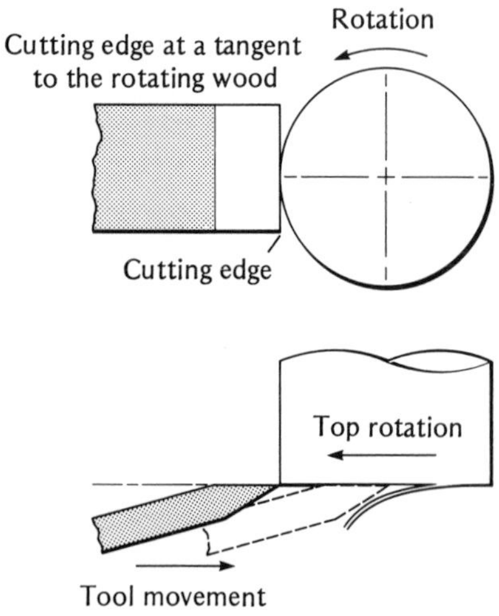

On the lathe it is the wood that is moving and the cutting edge is stationary, almost the reverse of the bacon slicer. The situation where it occurs is when cutting on a radius, and the cutting edge is at a tangent to that radius and pointing towards the axis. As the wood yields very little, there is a limit to the depth of the cut that can be made in the centre of a piece of wood. Making a small cut there produces no shavings. The slicing cut is best made close to the ends, where the slices must be very thin so that they will yield to allow the cutting edge to pass through.

The slicing cut can only be made in one direction, radially, which

Fig. 2.11

Slicing cut

Cutting edge at a tangent to the rotating wood

Rotation

Cutting edge

Top rotation

Tool movement

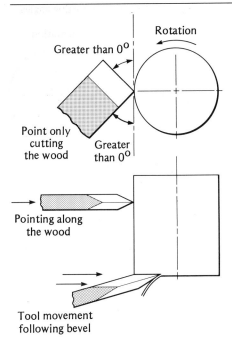

Pointing at the end of the wood. Note the clearance angle created between the long cutting edge and the wood by the angle of the tool.

Fig. 2.12 Pointing cut with the chisel

is at 90° to the shear. Peeling cuts along the surface parallel to the axis.

Pointing

The pointing cut is similar to the slicing cut in that it cuts between two parts of the wood and separates them. The cutting is by a sharp point piercing the wood as would a nail or a pin, but by virtue of the rotation of the wood and slow feed of the point, the wood is pierced all the way round. In the centre of a piece of wood there is a limit as to how deep it can be pierced because the wood yields very little. When the piercing is near the edge then the thin section of wood does yield and allows the piercing to proceed deeper and deeper.

The cutting action is not as clean as slicing and the waste side is pushed away by the following bevel, usually breaking it into small fragments when working on end grain. But it can produce long, feather-like waste when working along the grain. The pointing cut is independent of direction.

Peeling plus Slicing

Peeling and slicing are the two basic forms of cutting with the same acute edge. Both forms are very different and are applicable at 90° to each other. Now that is fine if those were the only situations in which we were to turn, but that is not the case. Most cutting will be between

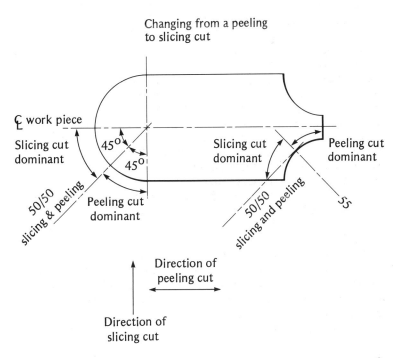

Fig. 2.13

those situations, which does not conform precisely to either one or the other form of cutting.

If we assume, in moving round a curved surface from one extreme to the other, that the optimum method of cutting gradually changes from shear peeling parallel to the axis, to slicing at 90° to the axis (and vice versa).

To try and analyse the situation let's look at what is happening to the type of cutting when working round this curve. The cut at the start is shear peeling with whatever angle of shear is preferred, (say 45°). As we start to move around then the type of cut gradually changes, but for the first 45° the shear peeling cut is dominant. At 45° the type of cut is 50/50, shear peeling/slicing. From 45–90° slicing cut is dominant and becomes totally a slicing cut at 90°.

To accommodate this change in the type of cut, the presentation of the cutting edge has to change with the direction of the cut. We know the tool positions at the start and the finish so it is just a matter of gradually changing from one to the other. In practice I have found that the angle of shear should be increased to 90° shear at the half way stage; through the second half the edge should be set for a slicing cut.

What we have been talking about here is the 'cutting edge' of a tool, (not scraper) which is cutting the finished face. It is independent of type of tool, independent of whether you are spindle or bowl turning on the inside or outside. This is a general procedure to follow for the best possible finish on the wood.

The cutting edge we have been talking about could be on the deep fluted gouge, skew chisel or shallow fluted gouge because they are all presented to the wood in the same way for the best finish. You could pick up any of those tools and make a fine cut with the tip of the tool in precisely the same way.

In practice, there are differences in tool characteristics, and access to the shape being cut. The wood also has preferences in direction of cutting. Combining these with the basic procedure above gives us turning practice.

Cutting and the tools

The four methods of cutting described are all used with standard wood turning tools. Some of them are easily identified with particular tools and are self explanatory but the situation can be a little complex so this section identifies which of the cutting methods are used by the various tools.

Chisels

The chisel is basically an acute cutting edge which will either peel, shear peel or slice, including all variations in between. The descriptions given so far directly relate to this tool. The other type of cut it performs is pointing. Either of the two sharp corners at the ends of the cutting edge are used.

Scrapers

In this case the title tells us precisely the type of cutting this tool performs. No additional description is needed.

Gouges

All the methods of cutting described have been performed with either the chisel or scraper, but most of the wood turning tools used are called 'gouges'. Where do these fit in with the methods of cutting wood?

Defining how a gouge cuts the wood isn't straightforward, as it is very much a function of the shape of the flute and the way in which the edge is shaped, sharpened and presented to the wood.

Flutes are made in two basic forms, shallow and deep. Methods of shaping, sharpening and using are down to personal preferences and the individual quirks of the craftsmen.

Deep fluted gouge

Take the case of the deep fluted gouge, I grind the bevel anywhere between 45–60°, the edge taken back along the tool from $\frac{1}{2}$–1 in and the tip has a curve and the bevel angle can vary around the cutting edge.

Presenting the tool square onto the wood with the bevel tangential to the surface we can see that the tip of the tool will 'peel' off the shavings. What precisely the rest of the edge would do in this attitude is dependent on how the bevel runs around the cutting edge. It isn't usually possible to go very deep in this attitude because the tool is much wider than the cutting edge and the bevel around the cutting edge will prevent contact between cutting edge and the wood before the depth of cut has reached about $\frac{1}{8}$ in.

Fig. 2.14 Deep fluted gouge set horizontal with bevel parallel to axis

As in the case of the chisel, to be able to work along the surface, the tool should be twisted round so that the tip is in a shear peeling position with the cutting edge pointing along the wood. In making this move with the deep fluted gouge, I bring the tool handle to the horizontal position, point the bevel in the direction of travel and twist the tool to give the tool the required angle of shear.

Depending on how much the tool is twisted, the cutting actions of the tip and the sides of the flute change. With the flute verticle, the centre of the flute is horizontal and therefore in a scraping position. The sides of the flute in this position are almost vertical and would peel if the bevel did not prevent it. Twisting the tool 45° brings the tip to a shear peeling cut with a shear angle of approx 45°, the sides of the flute will be at approx 55° to the vertical and in the change over region between peeling and scraping. Twisting the tool further until the lower flute is at 90° to the vertical it will be in a true scraping position. The centre of the flute will be in a 80° shear peeling position.

Take a very close look at the similarity in cutting actions between *(Figs. 2.12* and *2.13)*. Once we understand the situation, we can vary the shear peeling and scraping actions by twisting the tool to give us the optimum cutting angle for any particular operation. The tip can be set to shear peeling angle for the best possible finish. The side of the flute set for efficient waste removal by rotating the tool until the cutting action along the flute is prevented by the bevel. Just before this point is the optimum position for efficient waste removal, be it scraping or peeling, depending on the angle of the bevel at that point which will vary with depth of cut as the bevel may spiral slightly. For many operations a compromise between the two may be best.

That is fine when working parallel to the axis. From the chisel section we know that at 90° to the axis the shear peeling cut is replaced with the 'slicing cut'. The situation for the tip of the gouge, i.e. precisely the same as the chisel, as we move round from parallel to square to the axis is that the shear angle should be increased to 90° half way round and remain at that until in the fully slicing cut. The side of the flute will still cut all the way round.

When used horizontally the tip of the deep fluted gouge will give a good finish from a shear peeling cut or the slicing cut, while the lower side of the gouge flute will remove waste efficiently by the scraping or peeling action. It is a very versatile tool.

Shallow fluted gouge

The shallow fluted gouge fits somewhere between the deep fluted gouge and the chisel. Depending on the shape of the flute, how it is shaped, sharpened and presented to the wood it can also cut by scraping, peeling, slicing or by a combination of actions.

The small shallow fluted gouges are similar to deep fluted gouges, while the large shallow fluted gouges are much more like bent chisels and for all practical purposes should be regarded as such.

TURNING TOOLS

Turning tools can basically be described as sections of steel supplied by a manufacturer, sharpened at one end by the turner with a handle fitted at the other.

Standard Tools

There are three main categories: gouges, chisels and scrapers.

Gouges are defined by the shape and size of the flute, while chisels and scrapers use the width of the rectangular bar and the shape of the cutting edge to describe different types. Gouges and chisels are very general tools. They perform most of the cuts required in turning and many items can be turned completely with one or the other, and can achieve a finish that requires minimal, if any, sanding. Scrapers on the other hand are a specific tool, the ends sharpened in a particular shape to suit a form. Some shapes will be used on a number of jobs while others will be ground for an individual project. Scrapers

Fig. 3.1 Tools of the trade. A selection of Sorby high speed steel tools

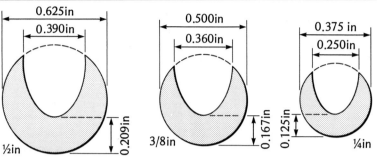

Fig. 3.2

Sorby high speed deep fluted gouges round section

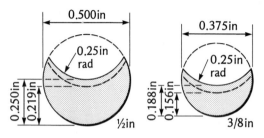

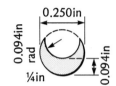

Sorby shallow fluted gouges long and strong

Dotted line represents standard gouge round section

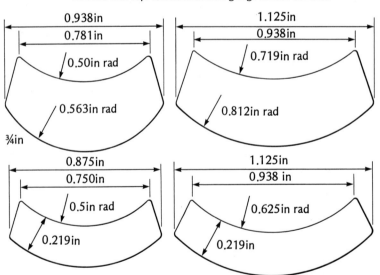

Forged section shallow fluted gouges.
Upper long and strong, lower standard

are also used extensively by pattern makers and musical instrument makers because they can achieve dimensional accuracy not possible with any other tool.

Most of the tools available up to the mid-70s were made from carbon steel, many hand forged by skilled craftsmen. The material has served the turner very well for generations but is now in the process of being superseded by more suitable steels. The biggest drawback with carbon steel is that it is relatively soft; this meant that the sharp cutting edge became blunted very quickly, requiring regular visits to the grindstone. Modern high speed grinders without a cooling fluid also contributed to the material's downfall because the temperature at which the carbon steel lost its temper is very easily reached, further reducing the life of the cutting edge and the tool.

High speed steel overcomes both of these problems to some extent because it is much harder and the temperature at which it loses its temper is considerably higher. At the same time as HSS was introduced so were new manufacturing methods, with many of the gouges being machined from standard round sections where possible. This move has led to a little confusion on the sizing of the gouges, the shallow fluted ones using the bar diameter, while the deep fluted use a size between the bar diameter and the width of the flute. It does not matter too much just as long as you know what you are buying.

HSS has not yet swept the board because the price is around double that for the equivalent carbon steel tool, even though manufacturers claim that they last up to six times longer. Tools of both materials are being marketed along side each other.

Tungsten carbide is also creeping into turning tools, but mainly for the tips of scrapers and with limited availability at present. It is much harder than HSS and takes a very sharp edge, though I am led to understand that it does not take a burr.

Having tools of various materials has its drawbacks because ideally they each require a different kind of grindstone. As most of the tools I use are made by 'Sorby', who are by far the biggest turning tool manufacturers in the UK, I will use their range of HSS tools to illustrate what is available.

Deep fluted gouges.				$\frac{1}{4}$″	$\frac{3}{8}$″	$\frac{1}{2}$″			
Shallow fluted gouges,									
Round stock	$\frac{1}{8}$″	$\frac{1}{4}$″	$\frac{3}{8}$″						
Forged stock				$\frac{1}{2}$″	$\frac{3}{4}$″				
Roughing gouges				$\frac{3}{4}$″		$1\frac{1}{4}$″			
Chisels, rectangular stock									
(all shapes)				$\frac{1}{2}$″	$\frac{3}{4}$″	1″	$1\frac{1}{4}$″		
Super skew, oval stock					$\frac{3}{4}$″	1″			
Scrapers (all shapes)			$\frac{3}{8}$″	$\frac{1}{2}$″	$\frac{3}{4}$″	1″	$1\frac{1}{4}$″	*2″	

*carbon steel only

Parting tools:

Standard $\frac{1}{8}$″, $\frac{1}{4}$″, Diamond section $\frac{3}{16}$″. Beading and parting $\frac{3}{8}$″.

There are also cranked parting tools, scrapers with removable HSS tips, round and diamond side-cutting scrapers. 'Long and strong' means just that when applied to carbon steel tools, but just means long for HSS tools. The carbon steel range is very similar but are usually forged, giving different outer profiles to the gouges.

Handles

The handle is a very important part of the tool, without it any tool would be very difficult, if not impossible, to use. It's the equivalent of the boat's tiller or the steering wheel on a car. A very small wheel or tiller would make directional control very hard work and imprecise, while a very large one would be very clumsy indeed (though requiring much less force). The steering system has to be balanced for the easy use of the driver or crew and has to match the size and weight of vehicle and the use to which it is being put.

The handle needs just as much consideration to make a balanced and easy-to-use tool. By balance I do not mean weight, i.e. pivoting the tool on the ferrel to see if the handle balances the stock. Doing that will help to pass the time but nothing else. It is the forces on the tool that are to be balanced when pivoting on the tool rest, so that the force required on the handle to balance the cutting forces on the tip is a reasonable working force and does not detract from the control of the cutting. A strong man can work with shorter handles than the average but don't get macho about handle sizes.

There are no definite rules about handles but the following considerations will help as a guide:

1. It must be capable of holding the tool securely.
2. The heavier the tool the heavier and longer the handle, and vice versa.

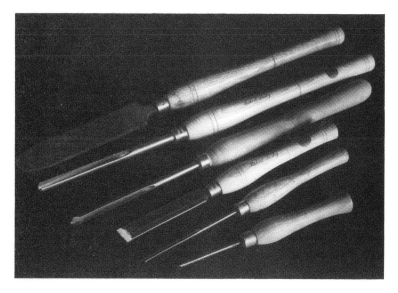

Fig. 3.3 Tool handles

3. The handle needs to be long enough to make overcoming the downwards cutting forces on the tip easy, even when working at the maximum overhang from the rest. Bear in mind that the forces on the end of a scraper are much greater than on the gouge.
4. 'If it looks and feels right then the chances are that it will be right' is often a good design rule. But since everyone's ideas are different it is one that I would discard. Substitute 'the proof of the pudding is in the eating'. Be prepared to change handles sizes to find the right one.
5. Remember that the length of the tool will reduce with use by as much as 4–6 in over its life time, which means the balance of the tool will change.

This is a selection of what I consider suitably balanced handles for standard tools. They are generally larger than the manufacturer's suggestions.

Description	Size	Handle length
Deep fluted gouges	$\frac{1}{2}''$	18″+
	$\frac{3}{8}''$	15″
	$\frac{1}{4}''$	12″
	$\frac{1}{8}''$	12″
Shallow fluted gouges	1″	15″
	$\frac{3}{4}''$	12″
	$\frac{1}{2}''$	10″
	$\frac{1}{4}''$	10″
Roughing gouges	$1\frac{1}{4}''$	15″+
	$\frac{3}{4}''$	12″
	$\frac{1}{2}''$	12″
Scrapers and chisels	2″	20″+
	$1\frac{1}{2}''$	18″
	1″	15″
	$\frac{1}{2}''$	12″
	$\frac{1}{4}''$	10″

For miniature or extra large turning, handles need to be adjusted to suit.

Shaping the cutting edge

Before we approach the grinder to shape the cutting edge of the tool, we must have a pretty good idea of what we want. Angles, within limits, are not as important for the cutting as they are for access, an extra 10° will make some difference to the performance of the skew but it significantly alters the shape of a 'V' or the angle between two beads on the object into which the skew can fit. Sure a fine cutting edge will produce better results but it's more difficult to grind and can be very quickly destroyed. A heavy angle will last longer and can be compensated for by the angle at which it is presented to the wood. Fine angles also produce long bevels which make form control more difficult, particularly on coves and concave shapes.

Don't forget that the angle of the cutting edge with a concave, unhoned edge, is less than the average bevel angle, particularly with long bevels and small grinding wheels, an effect which is doubled on the chisels.

The shape of the cutting edge is important because it defines how any part of the edge will contact and cut the wood, hence the range of basic stock from which the tools are made to cover many different operations and situations. The edge on each of the stock shapes is ground for efficient cutting, access to shapes, good finishing and to create clearance so that corners and parts of the tool not being used are well away from the wood.

When it comes down to it, there is a fair degree of personal preference. One shape or angle is not necessarily better than another, it's just a matter of how you use the tool and what you feel happy with. That is what is best for you. On the other hand don't be inflexible, approach the subject with an open mind and be prepared to at least try other suggestions. Stock shapes have changed over recent years and at the same time the shapes to which they are ground have evolved rapidly and are continuing to do so.

Most of my turning has been with the deep fluted gouge so it has had greater opportunity to evolve. Some changes were made deliberately, other happened by accident on the grindstone. This tool has now influenced how I shape, sharpen and use all the others, and the process continues.

Fig 3.4

Effect of hollow grinding on a chisel

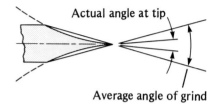

Actual angle at tip

Average angle of grind

Shaping and sharpening

Tool sharpening is not only an important but an essential part of turning, a part which it is well worthwhile giving careful consideration to before starting. Turning tools are usually shaped and sharpened on a bench grinder, which is be far the most popular form of powered grinder used by turners.

Think of the grinder as a lathe, the similarities are quite surprising. There is a motor which is probably more powerful than the lathe's but not continiously rated. This drives round at about 3000 rpm two wheels of compound which we wear down with our tools. (A slight exaggeration there). There is a tool rest which can be adjusted to suit particular tools and the changing diameter of the wheels. The wheels get dirty and misshapen and require a special tool to tidy them up, called a 'wheel dresser'. This further reduces the wheel diameters. The only important part of the operation is the contact made between the tool tip and the wheel with the product being a well-shaped and sharpened tool.

Knowing which grinder to buy isn't easy. It's far too tempting just to buy any grinder which looks nice and suits our pockets without really thinking about what we need. Most of the tools work well and hone easier with a slightly concave bevel, but not too concave. A 6–8 in diameter wheel would be suitable for most tools. Any smaller and the shape would be too severe. Any larger, though acceptable in terms of the grind, would be getting into industrial equipment and beyond the reach of our finances. For width I would suggest 19–30 mm as being reasonable for the size of tools to be ground.

The motor should be powerful enough for the job, around 0.5 kw minimum on a 6 in wheel, more on a bigger one. With two wheels we would want two different grits, a course grit for roughing and shaping, a fine grit for sharpening. The type of grit and bonding compound should match the material to be ground. Until recently all turning tools were made from a hardened carbon steel for which the 'grey' wheels were right. With high speed steel and with the tungsten carbide tipped tools introduced in the late 1970s, different grinding wheel materials and compounds are needed. The harder the steel, the softer the binding compound to be used. Wheels are colour coded, grey for carbon steel, white for HSS and green for tungsten carbide. Changing from one type of wheel to another takes some getting used to. The softer wheels wear away much more quickly and are prone to hollowing when grinding gouges. This creates a slight problem with the gouges but a much bigger problem when sharpening chisels. The answer is to pay greater attention to the condition of the wheels and to dress them regularly. If, like me, you have a mixture of carbon and HSS tools then you won't go far wrong with the grey wheels.

As with turning, different tools will be presented to the wheels at different angles, and in the case of gouges the angle will vary around the edge. The tool rest needs to accommodate all the tools with a minimum of adjustment and preferably none at all. The best rest is a narrow rounded edge, parallel with the face of the wheel, about 1 in longer on each side and set above the axis.

This will provide support for the tool very close to the wheel making control of the grinding as easy as possible. Unlike turning, the rest could also be used as a guide when sharpening chisels and scrapers. If you feel the need to use some sort of jig for some tools, then position it so as not to foul others.

Placing the grinder in the right position and at the right height are both important. It should be as close as possible to the lathe to encourage regular visits and at a height for easy use. From my own experience the centre of the grinder should be approx 3 in above elbow height. This is a comfortable working position, with good visibility without stooping.

With the right grinder in the right location and at the right height we can now think about using it. Again, it is like turning. Where do we stand? How do we hold the tool? The same problems, but there are slightly different solutions. We know that the tip of the tool won't be moving far but the handle could swing round almost 180°. We need to be in a position where we can see the grinding action and have precise, firm control over the tool movement. All the forces are very light. As most of the tools will be 16–24 in long, it would be difficult to stand directly in front of the wheel. I find standing slightly to

Fig. 3.5 Grinder set at elbow height and standing to one side, for good visibility and flexibility of tool movement

Fig. 3.6

Initial contact between tool and grindstone

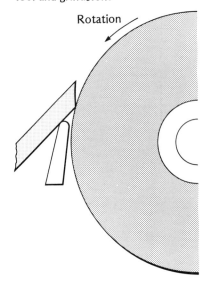

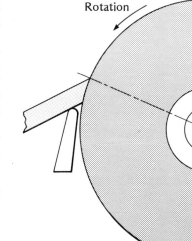

the side, looking across the wheel gives me the visibility and freedom of movement, without my body getting in the way of the swinging handle. The side will depend on whether you are left or right handed. The type of grip depends on the tool. A square ended scraper can be held with the full hand because there is very little movement. The deep fluted gouge needs a big swing with almost 120° of twist; for this a light hold in finger tips, in which the tool is rolled, allows the complete movement with ease. A finger tip hold works well for most of the tools.

The grinder performs two functions, it sharpens the tools, usually by following the existing form, and it shapes, which is the same action as sharpening but lingering in areas where more metal is to be removed.

At the beginning of this section we have defined a basic shape of the cutting edge and the form of the bevel for each type of tool. At the grinder we need to follow these shapes methodically and consistently or too much time and metal will be wasted in correcting mistakes.

Fig. 3.7

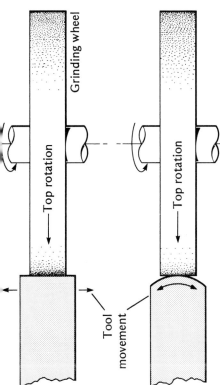

The approach to the grinder is the same for all tools, place it on the rest, square to the wheel, bring the heel of the bevel into contact with the wheel then raise the handle until the whole of the bevel between the heel and the edge makes contact. This can be judged by feel, by seeing just a few sparks beginning to bounce on the tool, or alternatively using a pre-set angle on a jig or guide.

Scrapers

Scrapers are relatively easy to sharpen with the main aim of putting a burr on the tip which is to do the cutting. The burr needs to be sharp. The only way to ensure this is to completely remove the old burr, first by rubbing a flat slip stone over the top surface of the scraper ready to make a clean start on a new one. Once this is done, sharpening can commence, placing the tool on the rest and when set at the required angle, swinging the handle to grind round a curve or sliding it along the rest for a flat edge. Do not sharpen for too long as the tool will be wasted unnecessarily and the burr will build up too large, bend over and become too brittle for use. A new, clean, small burr is what is required.

Gouges

Gouges are more complicated because the form is much more complex, and everyone grinds their gouges differently. Start with the easy one, the roughing gouge. This is ground with a 45° bevel and is square across the end. If you think of it in two sections, for the centre which is circular, the action to follow the flute is achieved by twisting the tool. For the sides of the flute which are flat, when the twisting action brings them to the horizontal position then the movement changes to sliding the tool across the wheel.

This procedure produces a square profile because the flute and the outside curve are concentric circles. [The deep fluted gouge and the larger, forged, shallow fluted gouge which are also concentric, (or as near as makes no difference) will also produce a square profile when ground in this method.]

Sharpening the roughing gouge

Gouge is slid across the grindstone over this area

Gouge is twisted over this area

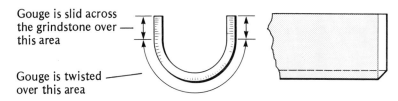

Fig. 3.8

Fig. 3.9 Grinding the 1¼ in roughing gouge, flat edge horizontal on the stone

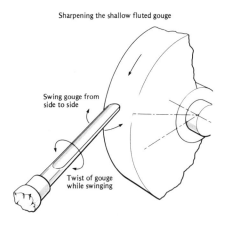

Sharpening the shallow fluted gouge

Swing gouge from
side to side

Twist of gouge
while swinging

Fig. 3.10

Grinding the flute in this shape involves three actions to be made:
1. The tool is twisted approximately ±65° to the vertical.
2. The tool is swung from side to side approximately ±60° to the line of the wheel.
3. The handle is raised and lowered approximately 30° below the start position as the grinding is taken along the flute.

All these movements put together will give the correct grind, providing the form is right to start.

The larger forged shallow fluted gouges are suitable for grinding with a shallow curve at the end. The movement can either be swinging from side to side only, twisting only, or a combination of the two. The plan and side profiles can all be the same but the bevel angles will be different towards the edges. All three shapes are OK.

For the shallow fluted gouges from round stock, a more rounded end is appropriate. Grinding with only the swinging or twisting movement produces a concave profile to the cutting edge where it should be convex or possibly flat. Combining a little twisting with the swing, or a little swing with the twist will produce the desired result.

Sharpening the shallow fluted gouge

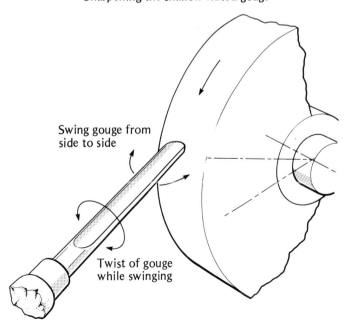

Swing gouge from side to side

Twist of gouge while swinging

Fig. 3.11

The deep fluted gouge ground square across, as the roughing gouge, is rather a clumsy and possibly dangerous tool, especially if the corners become entangled in the wood. The tool becomes much more versatile and user-friendly if the corners are ground back along the flute. Using the twisting action only gives a good working shape for which Geoff Parsons[2] designed a simple grinding jig. My preference is to grind the corners much further back to the point where the cutting edge almost blends in with the edge of the flutes. This increases the length of the cutting edge, making a tool that can take a very large cut (usually limited by the motor size).

Deep fluted gouge

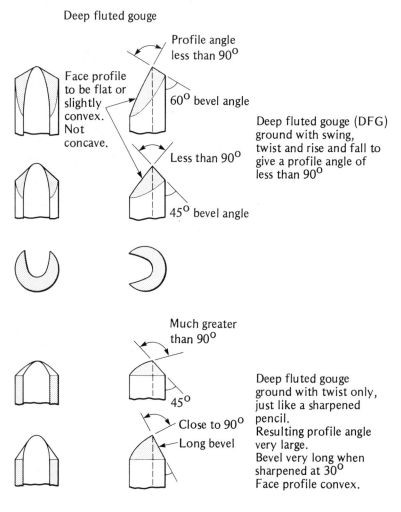

Profile angle less than 90°

Face profile to be flat or slightly convex. Not concave.

60° bevel angle

Deep fluted gouge (DFG) ground with swing, twist and rise and fall to give a profile angle of less than 90°

Less than 90°

45° bevel angle

Much greater than 90°

45°

Close to 90°

Long bevel

Deep fluted gouge ground with twist only, just like a sharpened pencil. Resulting profile angle very large. Bevel very long when sharpened at 30° Face profile convex.

Fig 3.12

Chisels

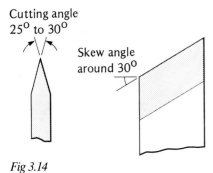

Cutting angle
25° to 30°

Skew angle
around 30°

Fig 3.14

Chisels

In general, chisels require much more care in grinding because both faces are ground leaving no reference edge, and the tool angle, which can be very acute, with very sharp points, is more liable to overheat and burn the edge and corners.

The chisel is placed on the tool rest with the cutting edge horizontal and the heel of the bevel on the wheel. Raise the handle to give the correct angle, then slide the tool horizontally backwards and forwards on the wheel and rest, keeping the tool at a constant angle and

Fig. 3.13 Sharpening a skew, cutting edge is kept horizontal on this side and again when the chisel is turned over to sharpen the other side

the edge horizontal. Repeat on the other side. The tool rest needs to be both horizontal and parallel to the face of the wheel for this method.

A curved skew is ground by setting the centre of the cutting edge horizontal on the wheel when swinging the handle from side to side, pivoting in the fingers at the centre of the curve, until the required form is obtained.

After initial sharpening on the grindstone and the removing of the burr on an oil stone, subsequent sharpenings of the chisel can be made very quickly on the oil stone until the flat parts of the bevel become wide. This makes oil stoning slow. The process can be started again on the grinder. Many of the parting tools are similar to chisels and are sharpened in the same way. Any other tools will fit into one of these categories.

Fig. 3.15 Removing burr after sharpening, or 'secondary' sharpening

Slip stones

All this grinding has produced 'burrs' on the edges of all the tools. What are we to do with them? Leave it on the scrapers because it improves the cutting action. Take it off the chisels with either a slip stone or oil stone, because it spoils the cutting edge. So what do we do with the gouges when they scrape, slice and peel all on the one cutting edge? The academic answer would be to remove the burr selectively. Mine is to leave it on unless I am unhappy with the finish, then I take it all off.

Over 90% of problems on the lathe are to do with the cutting edge of the tool. A good motto is 'when in doubt, re-sharpen'. If the problem persists:

(a)   resharpen,
(b)   dress the grind stone and resharpen,
(c)   have a cup of tea and resharpen.

26

CUTTING THE WOOD

As it prefers to be cut

From the objectives listed in Chapter 2, there is one which relates specifically to cutting the wood:

'To produce a good clean surface.'

This is achieved by 'cutting the wood as it prefers to be cut' as Frank Pain said, working with the grain of the wood to produce the best possible finish.

The easiest way to start is to consider working a flat piece of wood as a cabinet maker or joiner would do. The plane, chisel, spoke shave, etc are the tools which will resemble the peeling cut of the chisel.

From practical experience we know that planing a piece of wood

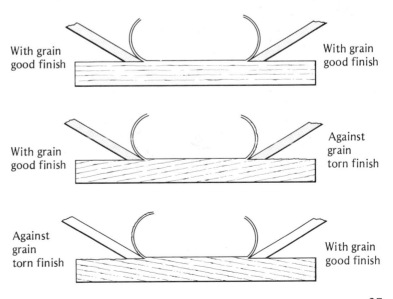

Fig. 4.1 Effect of grain and cutting direction on surface finish

27

across the grain results in torn grain and a poor surface. Working along the grain gives a much improved surface, but this depends on precisely how the grain runs through the wood. If it is perfectly parallel to the surface being worked then the direction makes very little difference, (except with particular types of wood). If the grain runs slightly across the thickness of the plank and portrudes through the surface, then the direction of planing is critical. Working with the grain is to work in the direction the grain is running as it comes to the surface. Going the opposite way will tear the grain and leave a poor finish. So, a piece of wood with cross grain needs to be worked in opposite directions on each side.

Working on end grain presents different problems. On a square end it doesn't make too much difference in which direction the surface is worked as all of them are difficult, requiring very sharp tools to cut a clean surface. We can start a cut at one side and work across the surface. As the tool approaches the opposite edge the last few grains, which have no support behind them, break away. The deeper the cut the more the breakaway. The situation can be improved by either providing support at the back of the wood or always working from the edge towards the centre. Therefore end grain needs firm support behind it to be cut cleanly. To cut a chamfer on end grain it should be cut from the short to the long grains which will provide support. Going the other way is very difficult and will result in badly torn grain.

Cutting end grain

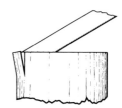

Cutting towards the edge. Grain is unsupported, breaking away.

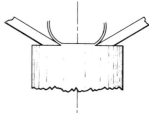

Cutting towards the centre. Grain supported.

Fig. 4.2

Cutting the wood on the lathe

Now put a piece of wood in the lathe, held between centres with the grain running along its length. Present the chisel to take a peeling cut and we are in trouble right away, as the rotation of the wood dictates the direction in which the wood meets the cutting edge. This is always circumferentially and is independent of grain direction. In this situation the cut is across the grain (from which we don't expect good results). The other way that wood is held for turning is across the grain, as when making bowls. Looking at the grain on the outside of a straight-sided bowl reveals a very complex situation. There is both side grain and end grain, which is continuously changing as the wood revolves. Consider the peeling action of chisel making a cut all the way round, now the side grain will be cut much as it prefers, along the grain as it is tangential to the axis. Some of the end grain will also be cut as it prefers, cutting from the short to long grain which supports it as it is cut. Around from that 90°, the end grain will be cut from long to short grain which will provide no support at all and produce a rough surface.

Both these turning situations result in the wood not being cut as it prefers with the consequent poor quality surface finish.

We can of course feed the cut in the preferred direction to improve the situation, but how much effect does this have? Consider turning an average 2 in diameter spindle. In making one revolution the cutting edge effectively covers 6.284 in, (the circumference). While

Fig. 4.3

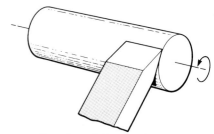

Rotation of the wood onto the cutting edge results in the wood being cut across the grain

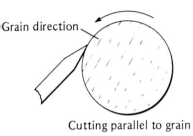

Grain direction

Cutting parallel to grain

Face plate turning

Cutting supported end grain

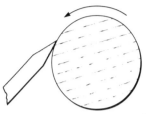

Cutting unsupported end grain

Fig. 4.4

Fig. 4.5

Effect of tool feed on cutting direction

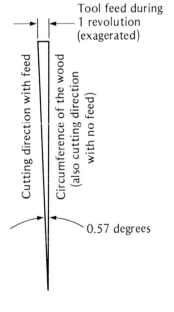

Tool feed during
1 revolution
(exaggerated)

Cutting direction with feed

Circumference of the wood
(also cutting direction
with no feed)

0.57 degrees

making that cut we would probably feed the tool along the surface approximately $\frac{1}{16}$ in (0.0625 in) giving a spiral cutting angle of 0.57°. This is a very negligible effect, which is even smaller on larger diameters. Therefore, the effect of the feed direction can be ignored when looking at how the wood is being cut.

Is there anything else we can do to improve the situation? Yes, there is, but a little bit of cunning and deception are necessary to fool the wood into thinking it's being cut as it prefers, the sort of thing you would expect from a pinball, snooker or billiards player. You will have seen them in the clubs or more likely on the TV, screwing the cue ball, playing lots of top, side or bottom to make the target ball think it has come from some other direction to which it then reacts. Take the situation in *Fig. 4.6*, and play for high scores, the black ball is in a direct line from the cue ball to the pocket. Now to pot the black, the cue ball is sent to hit the black 'square on', the black feels a force from that direction to which it reacts by moving towards the pocket and goes in. Such a straight shot is most undesirable in the game because the cue ball could follow the black into the pocket and there is little opportunity to position the ball for the following shot. A more desirable situation is for the cue ball to be to one side of that line, say position (b) *Fig. 4.6*. Now this looks a much more difficult shot because we have to judge just where to hit the black to make it follow the same path into the pocket as if it had been hit by the cue ball from position (a). The method is to hit the ball on exactly the same spot, the black ball will feel a force in the direction of the pocket and react by going in that direction into the pocket. If the cue ball were in position (c) then the procedure would be the same. Hit the black ball on exactly the same spot and we will get the same result. The shots from points (b) and (c) both fooled the black ball into thinking it had been hit from position (a). A simple enough trick and one which we can make use of in turning.

Just to prove how that works, let's play a little game. Consider a log of wood as a bundle of straws, a very simplistic view. This is more true of soft than hard woods, but it is an accurate enough analogy when planning how the wood is to be cut. Find a flat surface, a table or worktop will be ideal. Draw a line, approximately 12 in long, across the surface to represent the lathe axis. On the line stand six pencils (round pencils without a clip to represent the straws) 2 in apart to represent the end grain to be cut on the outside of a bowl.

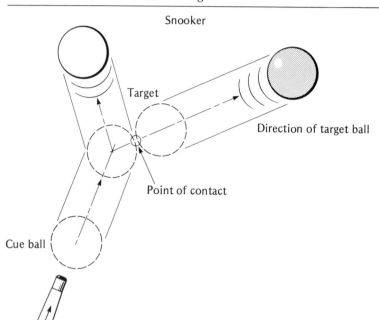

Snooker   *Fig. 4.6*

Target

Direction of target ball

Point of contact

Cue ball

Cue

Take a book, straight edge or magazine to represent the straight cutting edge of the chisel and hold it parallel to the axis at two thirds the height of the pencils. When you are ready, make a sharp jab at the pencils at 90° to the axis. This is just the same as if the wood (pencils) were rotating on to the chisel (book) in a peeling cut. If you are real macho they will all have fallen down. Now see how they are lying, They should be at 90° to the axis and the edge of the tool, which are both parallel. This represents the direction from which the end grain felt it was hit. This is exactly what we would expect. Turn the tool (book, etc) round to 30° to the axis to represent a shear angle of 30° and repeat the exercise. Remember to move the tool at 90° to the axis, exactly as before, as this represents the circumferential cut. This time the pencils should all be lying at 30° to the axis, i.e. 90° to the cutting edge. Try it again just to prove that it's not a trick.

Set up all the pencils on the line again with the tool at 30° to the axis, only this time move the tool in the sharp jabbing action *parallel* to the axis of the lathe. See how the pencils have fallen, at 90° to the cutting edge in exactly the same place as the previous test.

Before drawing any conclusions let's do one more test. Line up the pencils again with the tool (book) at 30° to the axis, only this time move the tool at 30° to the axis, (90° to the cutting edge). It should be of no surprise that they are all lying at 30° to the axis, 90° to the cutting edge.

So what does all that prove?

1. The pencils all fell down in line with the direction from which they perceived the force to come.

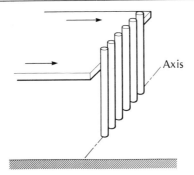

Effect of cutting edge direction
on grain reaction.
Experiment using pencils and book.

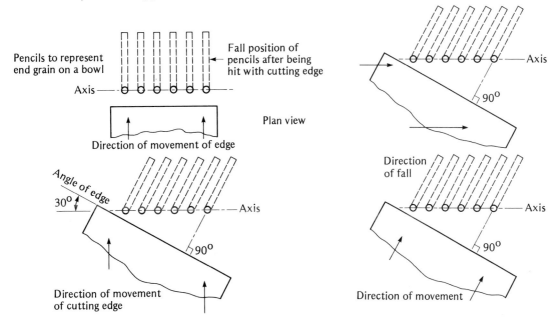

Fig. 4.7

2. The direction the pencils perceived the force to come from was
   independent of the direction of travel of the cutting edge.
3. The force was perceived to come at 90° to the cutting edge.
4. The direction the grain perceives the force to come from is the
   direction at which it thinks the cut is coming from.

This is leading us to an inevitable conclusion: The perceived direction of cut is independent of the direction of rotation and only
dependent on the direction that the cutting edge is facing.

Just to conclude, try a couple more tests. Set the pencils up again
and the cutting edge at around 75°, and move the cutting edge at 90°
to the axis. Avoid hitting the pencils with the side of the tool. You will
miss some, showing that as the angle is increased the width of the

cutting face is reduced. Now try it again with the edge at 90° to the axis. Unless you cheat a little the cutting edge will miss them all.

While these games have used a very simple model of wood, ignoring any bonding, etc, they do give us a valuable insight in to how to present the tool to the wood to cut it as near as possible to 'how it likes to be cut'. The tests established a principle which is equally valid whichever way the grain is running. It can be applied equally to spindle and bowl work.

Peeling cut

To relate this to the lathe: if the rotation of the wood onto a peel cutting edge, which is parallel to the axis, results in the wood being cut in an unsatisfactory direction, then the situation can be improved by altering the angle at which the cutting edge is presented to the wood, i.e. introducing the shear.

Looking at the piece between centres, the cutting edge should ideally be swung round to 90° shear to cut along the grain, but the cutting action is poor to non existent at this angle because none of the cutting edge is facing the rotating wood, so a lesser angle has to be used. There is absolutely nothing we can do about grain that is not parallel to the axis which requires cutting in opposite directions on opposite sides. We just take an average, which is parallel. That's fine for cuts parallel to the axis. For any other direction on the outside, the cutting edge should face from short to long grain which in this situation is from large to small diameter to cut with the grain. On internal surfaces, to work from short to long grain, the cutting edge should face from the small to the large diameter.

Looking at a bowl, if we turn the cutting edge right round to cut the end grain as it prefers, then the side grain will think it is being cut across the grain. Whatever we do will be a compromise. As the end

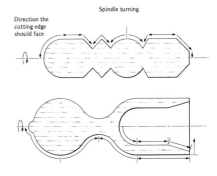

Fig. 4.8 Cutting the wood as it prefers to be cut

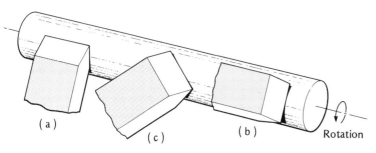

(a) Original position - cutting across the grain
(b) 90° shear cutting edge facing along the grain but not facing the direction of rotation. Therefore no cutting.
(c) Compromise position where cutting edge is partly facing the grain direction and partially facing the rotating wood

Fig. 4.9

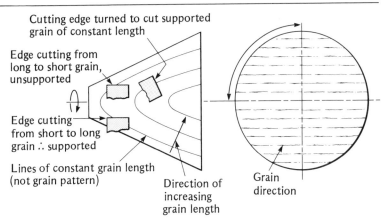

Cutting edge turned to cut supported
grain of constant length

Edge cutting from
long to short grain,
unsupported

Edge cutting
from short to long
grain ∴ supported

Lines of constant grain length
(not grain pattern)

Direction of
increasing
grain length

Grain
direction

Fig. 4.10 Bowl Turning

Direction the cutting
edge should face for
the end grain

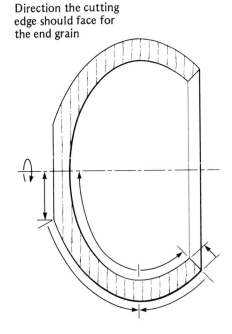

grain is likely to cause more trouble than the side grain then the compromise should favour the end grain. Say, a shear angle of 55–70°.

Let's take a more realistic example of a simple 'V' shaped bowl with an angle around 30° to the axis (above 45° the cut will be slicing.). Again, with the peeling cut, some of the end grain will be unsupported as before, but this time the grain to one side is shorter while the grain on the opposite side is longer. With a little studying we can draw lines of constant grain length all of which are for different lengths (a little like the isobars on the weather chart). This time in order to cut the end grain which is supported by grains of the same length, the direction of cut only need be moved round until the cutting edge is square to these lines, which is less than 90°. Turning it further, all the end grain on the bowl will be cut from short to long grain.

On the outside of a bowl the cutting edge should face from the smaller to the larger diameter, conversely on the inside it should face from the larger to the smaller diameter. While all this is theory, I have verified all the conclusions with a considerable number of tests on the lathe.

Slicing cut (above 45° to the axis)

The presentation of the cutting edge to the wood is a very specific position not leaving much room for manoeuvre. That does not matter, however. It is already fooling the wood into thinking the cut is being made radially, because the cutting edge is pointing towards the axis. Therefore, on end grain work, providing the cutting edge is facing from large to small diameter on the outside, the end grain is being cut precisely as it prefers, from short to long grain, and produces really excellent results. If used on the inside, which is rarely, then it should be facing in the opposite direction.

On bowls it will cut across the side grain, and from short to long end grain when it is facing from small to large diameters on the outside, and vice versa on the inside. This is obviously not ideal, but a very acceptable compromise.

Pointing

The situation with the pointing cut is much the same as the slicing cut in that it is already pointing to the axis. It is most often used on the outside where the angle of pointing can be adjusted slightly. In practice it gives a cleaner finish if raised 10–20° from the radial line.

Scraping cuts

Scrapers are presented to the wood in a very different way to a peeling tool. A scraper always lies flat on the tool rest so it is always cutting circumferentially and the cutting edge on the finished surface is parallel to the surface. In these circumstances the only possible way we can affect the cutting of the grain is the direction of feed. The tests we have done will not help us to analyse the situation. All we can do is to refer to practical experience, which suggests the following guide lines:

1. On spindle turning, feed from large to small diameter on the outside, feed from small to large diameter on the inside.
2. On bowl turning, feed from small to large diameter on the outside, feed from large to small diameter on the inside. In many cases feed direction does not effect the finish obtained. It is a matter of experience to find out when it does, as there are a considerable number of variables. There are instances, however, when the scraper can be twisted to shear cut position for a fine finishing cut. Unfortunately, the scraper is slightly unstable on the rest in this position.

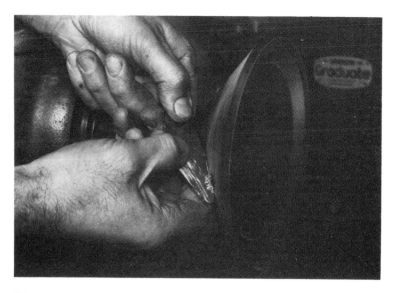

Fig. 4.11 Hand-held scraper removing a very fine shaving in a high shear position

There is a special scraper which is hand held without a rest, but this represents a very small proportion of the scraping in turning. The guide lines for this tool are similar to the peeling cuts.

The scraping does not cut the wood as it prefers to be cut. Therefore, its function as a finishing cut is limited to areas where access and control with other methods of cutting are limited, or where size tolerances are small. It can, however, produce an acceptable finish in many of these situations.

THE TURNER

Knowing how to shape and sharpen the tools, how they cut the wood and how the wood prefers to be cut, is only part of the story. The tool and the wood have to be brought together through the hands of the turner, which become the vital link in the process.

The hands hold, steady, and control the tool, but it is not just the hands that are involved, the arms, body, legs, feet, head and eyes, in fact almost every part of the body is included in the operation. Even with all that support, we do need a little more from part of the lathe, the tool rest. The whole process is totally dependent on the turner. We have to give every consideration to how and where we stand, how we hold and control the tool throughout the operation, ensuring that we are comfortable and in control at all times.

The tool rest

This is the only part of the lathe which I propose to consider. It becomes so involved with the actions of the turner, supporting his

Fig. 5.1. A good tool rest, straight-edged with a steep slope and room to hook a finger underneath

every move, that it is almost an extension of his hands. A poor or badly designed tool rest will make many of the operations unnecessarily difficult or even dangerous. Don't assume that because the rest was on the lathe when you bought it, that it is right. Take a very close look at what you have got or are about to buy. The tool rest, as the name implies, is a surface which supports the tool. It also provides a steady point for the support hand. It is *not* a guide to control the shape of the surface being cut. That is the function of the bevel on the wood.

The rest needs to be rigid, horizontal, movable (so as to be as close as possible to the wood) and adjustable in height $\pm \frac{3}{4}$ in from the axis height. The surface should be hard and smooth so that the tool can slide along it easily and support the tool close to the wood irrespective of its angle. It should not be too deep in section, as with certain grips the finger hooks round underneath it for delicate control and support. Long rests allow long cuts to be made, essential for form control, and also speed and efficiency. Short rests are useful in places with limited access but I often think that access could be improved if there was a short rest with the support to one side.

I use a straight rest which has always been adequate. Curved rests seem to be in vogue at the moment if the catalogues are to be believed. Their tops are usually flat, suggesting that they are specially for scrapers. Now that is OK if the scraper is to be perfectly horizontal all the time and not tipped slightly up or down, which is often necessary. Tipping the point upwards would bring the support point away from the wood. If the curve is to match inside bowls then tipping downwards will unbalance the tool by only supporting it at one point on the curve, which is not desirable for the scraper. If the rest is to match the outside curve then tipping slightly downwards, the support will be at the corners only which will dig in and prevent a smooth slide along the rest. I cannot see any reason at the moment for using one and certainly when learning they should be avoided.

Working heights

'What height should the lathe be set at?' is the wrong question. It should be, 'What is a comfortable working position?', for which there is no simple answer.

It depends on the type of turning being performed, which in the main can be split between spindle or bowl turning. When bowl turning, I like the tool handle to rest on the side of the hip when it is set horizontally, or just below with the tool on the rest which is at lathe centre line height. This gives me a great deal of flexibility in arm movement and also firmness and rigidity when necessary by holding it against the hip. To get this position, the lathe axis is around 2–3 in below my elbow. There will be some variation according to height. There is no definite rule but that is a good starting point. The spindle turning position is quite different; there is much more fine detail work with the tool at many different angles and for this I like the lathe to be 1 in or 2 in higher.

Fig. 5.2 The spindle turning lathe height is at or just below elbow height

If the lathe is to be used for both types of turning or by more than one person, then it should be set for spindle turning and the tallest turner. Plinths should be used to raise the heights of smaller operators and bowl turning. Don't forget that it's a good idea to have a plinth (even for the tallest) when working on a concrete or slate floor as these can be very cold to the legs and feet, even in a heated workshop. Once the lathe height is set, small adjustments can be made with plinths and by adjusting the tool rest height to get the working position comfortable.

Standing in line

Where do we stand in relation to the tool and how do we hold it. There is no doubt that to carry out all the cuts we must develop a degree of ambidextrousness. Don't fight this idea because it's not like trying to write with both hands, but more like eating. A right-handed person holds the fork in the left hand and the knife in the right. When using a fork only or spoon this is held in the right hand. Whichever hand the fork is in, it does exactly the same job, transfers food from the plate to the mouth. Most people have the necessary ambidextrousness without even thinking about it. That's the way it has to be with turning. Enter the workshop with a completely open mind and don't put any unnecessary restraints in your way.

Put a 12 in piece of 2 in by 2 in wood between centres in the lathe, put the rest at centre line height and pick up a $\frac{1}{2}$ in deep fluted gouge. ($\frac{1}{4}$ in or $\frac{3}{8}$ in will also do). The next step is very important: approaching the lathe with the tool. You could tuck it under your arm like a lance and approach the lathe as if in a jousting competition. With a good eye you might hit the wood, but it would not score you any points as turner. We must remember that the most important part of turning is the contact between the tip of the tool and the wood, everything else is arranged around this. We must know what result we want and plan a cut which will give us that result. For these first cuts, we want to reduce the square section to round. This requires cuts along the length from one end to the other. Stand about 3 ft away from the lathe, and holding the gouge out at arm's length place the end of it on the tool rest. We want to make a cut along the axis and we know that the bevel should point in the direction of travel. Keep the gouge horizontal with between 45–60° shear. Line up the bevel with the lathe axis pointing the tip in the direction of travel. The tip is now set in preparation to make the cut. Having set the tip, the position of the handle has also been set, it just remains now for us to position ourselves *around* the tool in a suitable position to be able to control the tool throughout the cut.

There are three factors to be considered in choosing this position:

1. Safety. If, as it sometimes does, the piece of wood (or splinters from it) decide to leave the lathe, then we want to be out of the line of fire. Also out of the line of fire of the wood shavings, as these can easily get into the eye.
2. Sight. Be in a position to see the cutting action at the tool tip and see the form being cut.
3. Continuity. Be in a position to complete the cut in one run (or as much as the tool rest will allow) without losing balance or getting the body in the way of the tool movement.

Now then, which way have you pointed the tool, towards the headstock or the tailstock? Just to make things easy for me let us point the tool towards the tailstock. Looking at the tool, three possible positions are suggested.

The first would be at the end of the handle. Here we are in line with the work and the shavings, and visibility is restricted. With a

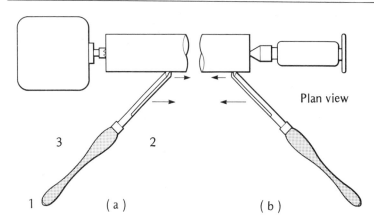

Fig. 5.3 Standing positions

Plan view

3   2

1   (a)   (b)

long handled tool (the one you are holding should be about 24 in in total), you will be too far away from the work to see what is happening and be in control.

The second position would be between the tool and the tailstock, with the tool pointing towards you. The handle would be held in the left hand (the control hand) and the stock in the right. The force required by the tool is a push along its length with the control hand. This is not too easy unless you are standing very close to the tool. When making the cut, the tool will move towards the body and at some stage will make contact with it. At which point some backwards movement (or sideways, depending on how you are standing) will be necessary to complete the cut. This is not the easiest way to move and retain balance and, therefore, complete control over the tool at the same time. To overcome this difficulty, we can position ourselves with the tool in the finish position at the end of the cut, then reach out to the start position for the cut to avoid the collision. This is uncomfortable and it is difficult to push the tool in the correct manner, the shavings are shooting right into your face and visibility is obscured. This can't be right.

The third position is behind the tool next to the headstock, with handle in the right hand and the stock in the left. The push required by the tool is easy to perform, we are looking down the direction of travel with a good view of the cutting action and the form of the wood, the shavings are going away from us, we are out of line of the wood and any flying splinters, and the movement for the cut is easy. Arm's length may be enough, but if not, the feet can be positioned so as to allow forward movement to retain balance and control for long cuts. (See over for positioning the feet.)

You may find that you are leaning on the headstock for extra balance and stability. That's very good and is to be encouraged. But you may find that the headstock was a bit of a nuisance and restricted the left arm position and movement. Also, if your lathe is a Harrison like mine, you will have switched it off with your hip at least half a dozen

Fig. 5.4 Standing in position: outside foot forward for balance and movement, left arm touching the headstock for stability, tool handle in right hand

times. This is a good time-saving trick when you are on production runs but far too often it is a nuisance.

This is a good position to work from and one which is essential for many jobs. There is of course a better alternative, turn the tool round to point from the tailstock to the headstock, and position yourself between the handle and the tailstock, facing the headstock with the right hip against the bed. The handle should be in the left hand and the stock in the right. (I tricked all you right handers). You are now looking down the direction of travel and the restriction of the tail-

Fig. 5.5 *Start of a cut: weight on back foot, inside foot forward, body in line with tool*

stock to the right arm is minimal. You are out of line of the wood, splinters and the shavings with good visibility and control. If your lathe is bench or cabinet mounted, you will be a little further away from the bed and consequently not so well positioned.

It's worth standing for a while and looking at the body and hand position relative to the tool as this will remain a constant throughout most of the turning. You should be standing behind the tool, and looking down the bevel in the direction of travel. That applies whether working from head (tool in right hand) or tailstock (tool in left hand).

42

Fig. 5.6 Standing in position when working from tailstock to headstock: tool in left hand, inside (right) foot forward, leaning forward towards end of cut, right hip against lathe bed for stability, body in line with tool

The problem we had with the headstock makes me think that all standard lathes are left-handed. What a thought!

We know where to stand and which way to face. It's now just a matter of how to place the feet. With both feet together, balance is limited and body movement impossible. Placing the feet wider apart, say 6 in improves the balance. If, at the same time, we put one foot in front of the other, this will allow us to move our body backwards and forwards, increasing the reach of our arms. Either foot could be the forward one, so try both positions. The advantage of putting the right foot forward when facing the headstock is that it places the body in line with the tool at the start of the cut. For the average cut,

Fig. 5.7 Working the outside of a bowl on a short bedded lathe

either can be used, starting with most of the body weight on the back foot and then transferring it to the front foot as the cut proceeds, thus maintaining balance and control throughout. On long cuts, or ones where there is a big swing of the handle (as in going round the outside of the bowl) this stance may not give us enough movement and we have to think in terms of moving the feet, or a foot, to maintain balance. As before, we start with the feet apart, most of the weight on the back foot at the start, transferring it to the front foot as the cut moves along. To move further forward, leave a small amount of weight on the back leg, thus maintaining the balance, then slide it forwards along the ground to a forward position where the body weight can be returned to it. Again either leg could be the one to move, but from my own experience balance and control are better maintained if the outside leg is the one that moves and the opposite hip can lean on the lathe bed. After all, on a long swinging cut it is the control arm on the outside which needs to be moved furthest.

Fig. 5.8 Bowl turning on a bedded lathe, sitting on the bed to be in the correct position behind the tool

Let's look at other turning situations and where to stand with the tool.

Bowl turning

1. Turning the bowl on the inboard side of a short bed lathe, i.e. no bed or tailstock in the way.
    a) bowl held on top surface while outer shape is turned. To work with the wood the cut is from the base to the rim. Place the tool on the rest to start the cut at the base and point the bevel in the direction of travel. Stand behind the bevel and the tool will be in the left hand.
    b) the bowl held on the base to work the inside. Place the tool

45

on the rest, point the bevel in the direction of travel and stand behind the bevel. To cut with the grain on the inside it is from rim to base.) This time the tool is in the right hand. The left hand can be used to support the bowl particularly when turning thin, or to reduce vibration if there is any.

2. Turning the bowl on the outboard end of the lathe, again with no tailstock or bed in the way.
   a) bowl held on top surface to turn outer shape. Tool on the rest at the base and bevel pointing from base to rim. Standing behind the bevel, the tool is held in the right hand.
   b) bowl held on the base to work the inside. Tool on the rest at the rim and pointing towards the base. Standing behind the bevel the gouge is held in the left hand.

3. Turning the bowl inboard on a bedded lathe.
   a) bowl held on top surface while outer shape is turned. Again the tool is on the tool rest at the base of the bowl and the bevel pointing in the direction of travel. We know to stand behind the bevel with the tool in the left hand but the bed and tailstock are in the way. If it's a relatively vertical bowl it may be possible to stand as for spindle turning, i.e. between the handle and the lathe bed. If that's tight then move over a little and sit on the bed to make room for the tool movement. When the bowl has a flatter profile, move around to the other side of the lathe for a comfortable position to turn from.
   With a bench mounted lathe these options are difficult, if not impossible. It may, therefore, be necessary to stand the other side of the tool to make the cut.
   b) bowl held on the base to work the inside. Place the tool on the rest with the bevel at the rim and pointing in the direction of travel. To work looking down the bevel the tool must be in the right hand.

Let us take two other situations. Making cuts at 90° to the centre line from rim to centre when the bowl is held on the top face.
   a) on the base.
   b) on the top

Q. Where should we stand?   **A.** looking down the bevel.

It's all a question of adopting a suitable standing (or sitting) position for the job being turned and the type of lathe. Don't be tied down by irrelevant conventions such as always 'standing' in front of the lathe and trying to do everything right (or left) handed. It will only make the job more difficult, if not impossible, and will be more dangerous.

The deep fluted gouge has been used to illustrate a suitable stance, so what about all the other tools? As we progress you will see that because of the similarities in the tools they require the same holding and standing techniques. Where it is different for particular operations then this is mentioned in that section.

Holding the tool

Knowing how to hold the tool might seem fairly obvious or, at least, not too critical. It is not quite so simple. In holding the tool we have to provide its stability, support and control, whether it is on a 2 ft diameter bowl or a tiny bead on a small spindle. The function of the grip is the same, but the method of the grip is different. When the work piece becomes thin or slender the grip has to be modified so that the hand can also support the wood.

The control hand needs an appropriate grip to carry out this function. Where there is no, or very little, twisting of the tool involved in the cut, then the grip is straightforward. The control hand holds the

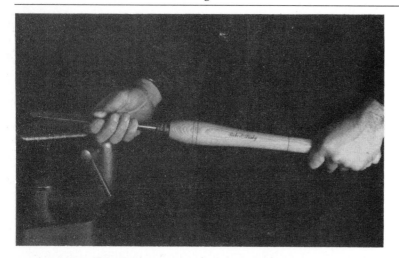

Fig. 5.10 Holding the gouge for a cut that does not involve rotating the tool 'control' hand with a full firm grip around the handle; 'steady' hand with a full underhand grip. The index finger may contact the steady . . . (author?) of a cut or for extra stability during cutting

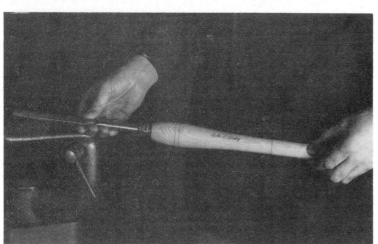

Fig. 5.11 Large gouge held in fingers of both hands so that it can be rolled easily. Steady hand in contact with the rest

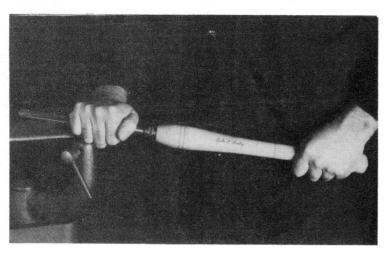

Fig 5.12 Both hands with a very firm grip. The steady hand overhand with palm against the rest for extra stability. This grip is particularly useful when starting with large, irregular bowl blanks

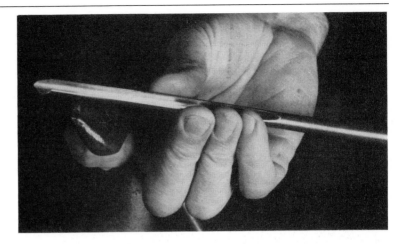

Fig. 5.13 Small gouge held in fingers and thumb for ease of rolling with the index finger hooked under the tool rest to act as an anchor for fine control. This is ideal for fine detail work where there is a large swing of the hands and only a small movement of the cutting edge

handle with the full hand and can look to the hip for additional support. Where there is twisting of the tool then the control should hold the handle between the fingers and thumb which can then roll the tool.

Steadying the tip of the tool is mainly achieved by pressing or pulling down on the tool to bring it into firm contact with the tool rest and prevent any vibration etc. Further steadying is gained by holding the bevel firmly against the wood. The grip can be anything from a light press on the top of the tool with the fingers through to heavy pressure with a full hand grip. In any of these cases the hand does not touch the tool rest. To support the tool on entry, the hand should be firmly pressed against the rest and the tool held in the fingers which can guide the tip forwards into the wood until bevel contact is obtained without the hand moving against the rest. The support can then continue as above. This method of support is also used in detail work such as V's and chamfers, the hand firmly against the rest and the tool held in the fingers which allow the tool to be pushed through them to complete the cut.

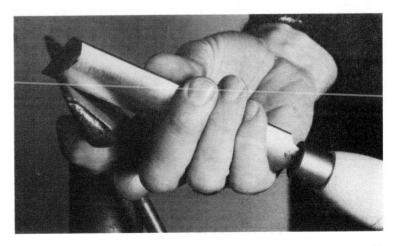

Fig. 5.14 Skew chisel held for squaring ends or shoulders of 'V's'. The hand can move forward with the tool

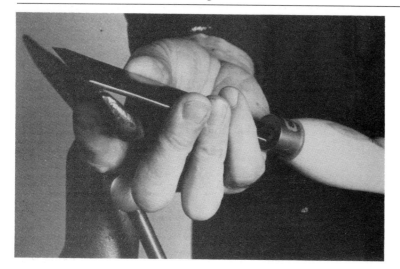

Fig. 5.15 Steady hand holding the skew at the start of a rolling cut (e.g. head). Tool held in fingertips with index finger hooked underneath the tool rest as an anchor

On other detail work such as beads and round corners where there is twisting of the tool and swinging of the handle, very firm support with flexibility is needed. The support is obtained by hooking the index finger under the tool rest and holding on like an anchor, then the tool is held in the tips of fingers and thumb which will allow the tool to be rolled and swung by the control hand. In the situation the steady hand also acts as a brake to prevent the tip from moving forward too quickly ahead of the handle movement.

The grip of the steady hand is modified in situations where the wood also requires support. In turning a thin bowl it is the inside that is finished last and therefore support is required on the outside of the bowl as the final cuts are made. The fingers are used to support the wood directly opposite the tool while the thumb either acts as a

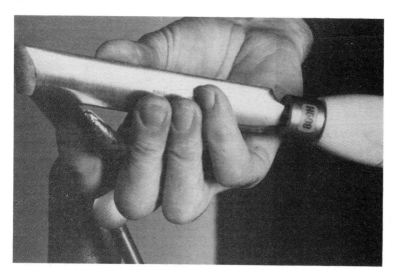

Fig. 5.16 The tool has completed the rolling movement

Fig. 5.17 Fingers supporting the bowl directly opposite the tool while the thumb acts as a backstop behind the gouge. Alternatively the thumb can rest on top of the gouge to provide support

backstop for the gouge on top of the rest or the thumb holds the gouge onto the rest. Either way, support is given to the wood at the same time as assisting the gouge.

Long thin spindles also require support while being cut to avoid buckling and breaking. In this situation it is advisable to minimise the buckling forces first, by slackening off the tailstock slightly. The fingers of the steady hand are wrapped around the spindle behind the tool and the thumb holds the tool down onto the rest, or onto the wood and rest as appropriate.

Alternatively, the thumb can act as a back support for the tool on the rest. The side of the hand may touch the rest for additional stability. While the steady hand is supporting the wood, the control can be brought to hold the handle at the ferrel end while the rest of the

Fig. 5.18 The fingers are first placed under the thin spindle for support, the tool is placed on the spindle and held there with the thumb. The control hand holds the handle near the ferrel with the handle supported under the arm and the index finger extended over the blade

handle is supported under the forearm. Of course there are many more situations requiring varied hand grips, but the above form the basis for many alternatives.

Control and stability

While the control and stability of the tools are obtained in similar ways, it is much better to look at the groups of tools separately. The principles of control and stability are best illustrated using the deep fluted gouge. The other tools can develop from there.

Deep fluted gouge

Both the stability of the tool and the cutting feed are obtained by a pushing action along the tool handle which brings the tool into a firm

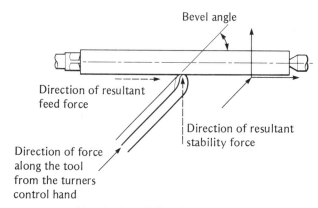

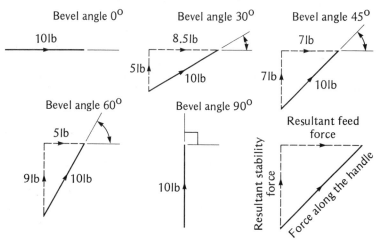

Fig. 5.19 Feed and stability forces

Fig. 5.20 Directional control on the bevel

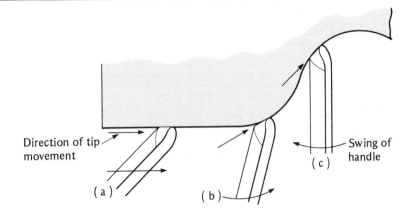

Direction of tip movement

Swing of handle

(a)

(b)

(c)

(a) Handle moved along at same rate as the tip giving a straight cut
(b) Handle gradually swung forward to give a convex curve
(c) Handle gradually swung backwards to give a concave curve
In all three cases pivoting is on the bevel

contact with the wood on the bevel. At this point the applied force is split into two components, one at 90° to the wood and bevel contact surface, which provides the stability of the tool by firm contact on the wood. The other component of the force is parallel to the bevel and the wood surface and moves the tool along the wood to give cutting feed. The proportion to which these forces are split is a function of the bevel angle. With a bevel angle of 90° all the force will be at 90° to the bevel, i.e. a very stable tool with no feed along the cut; a bevel angle of 0° and all the force will be parallel to the bevel. i.e. all feed and no stability force. At a bevel angle of 45° the force is split 50/50. If additional stability is required, this is provided by the support hand pressing the tool down on the rest.

Most of the forces on the tip of the tool from the cutting action are tangentially downwards and are easily resisted with downwards pressure on the long handle. The other forces, which are at 90° to that, are opposed by the push along the handle.

The bevel rubbing behind the cutting edge in the direction of travel is the key to form control and is also the point about which the tool is pivoted. It is very much like the control surfaces of a sailing boat, the keel providing the stability while the rudder at the stern gives directional control. The tool handle operates just like the tiller, being swung from side to side (pivoting on the same axis as the rudder), to change direction of the rudder, which in turn changes the direction of the boat. The direction of cut of the gouge is dictated by the direction the bevel is facing, this can be changed by swinging the handle either forwards or backwards to direct the bevel, and therefore the direction of cut, towards or away from the axis. The point of pivot for this action is the bevel which ensures a smooth continuous surface. Pivoting at some other point along the tool, say in the fingers of the steady hand tends to move the bevel away from the wood, therefore losing directional control and creating steps in the surface.

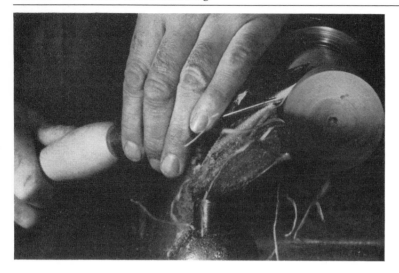

Fig. 5.21 Skew chisel. Steady hand pressing down on the tool to provide stability force to maintain a firm contact between the tool level and the wood

The chisel

The same basic principles also apply to the chisel, even though the tool's configuration is different and it is presented to the wood differently. The shear angle at which it is set makes a difference to the forces, as does the angle of skew and which way up the chisel is set. Trying to analyse these forces theoretically is very complicated and far beyond what we need. So we will look at the situation from a more practical viewpoint. With the skew chisel, the force along the handle not only provides a stabilising force and cutting feed, it also directly resists a large proportion of the cutting forces. Since the bevel angle is usually small (half the edge angle because it is sharpened on both sides), the stability component of the force is also small. Additional stability force from the steady hand which holds the chisel down firmly on both the tool rest and the wood is essential. This force also slightly resists the feed force, making control more positive.

Directional control is by two actions:

1. Swinging the handle forward (or backwards), pivoting on the bevel for the tool to go into the wood.
2. Twisting the tool to go into or out of the wood.

In most situations it is a combination, the method of cutting changing from shear peeling to slicing.

Shallow fluted and roughing gouges

These can be treated as the deep fluted gouge or skew chisel, depending on the bevel angles and how they are presented to the wood.

Scrapers

Stability for the scraper is obtained by holding it firmly flat on the tool rest, with a long handle to resist the downwards cutting force on the tip.

Directional control and cutting feed are both by drawing (or pushing) the cutting edge over the surface fairly lightly. The bevel may play a small part in the control but it is much more a matter of feel. The shape of the scraper is very important.

HOLDING THE WOOD

Holding the wood securely is one of the most important functions of the lathe, but the basic lathe does not do the job on its own. There are usually all sorts of attachments to fit to both the headstock and the tailstock.

In general wood is mounted on the lathe in one of two ways:

1. With the grain parallel to the lathe axis; this is usually called 'spindle turning'. Spindles, goblets, egg cups, boxes and so on are turned in this way.
2. With the grain running at 90° to the axis. This is usually referred to as 'bowl' or 'face plate turning'. Most pieces turned this way tend to be bowls, trays or similar objects.

If you are not careful in planning your turning, you can end up spending more money on chucks and holding devices than on the lathe itself. If you have plenty of money and are going to stick with the same lathe for a very long time, this is not a problem. However, many turners do progress and find that they would like a different

Fig. 6.1 Face plates, single screw chucks, drive centres and revolving centre

lathe at some stage. The chucks are unlikely to be compatible, and that is where the expense starts again.

Chucks are not always the magic solution they at first seem. I must admit that I was glad to see the end of screw holes in the bottom of bowls, but this euphoria didn't last too long. There seemed to be bowls everywhere with large dovetail recesses in the bases, which looked much worse than three neatly filled in screw holes. That was not the only problem. The size of the chuck often dictated the shape of many bowls: a 3 in diameter recess with another inch on top of that gives a 4 in base, which is much too large for a 6 in diameter bowl. This is not just the fault of the chuck but very bad planning and design.

The whole question of chucks — which, how, where and when to use them, and what their capabilities and limitations are, would almost fill a book on its own. All I want to look at here is the most basic methods of holding the wood for spindle and bowl turning.

Spindle turning

'Between centres' is the basic method of holding the wood: a drive dog in the headstock and a 'dead' or 'live' centre in the tailstock.

The drive dog has a centre, with two or four prongs which penetrate the wood, through which the power is transmitted. They are usually 1 in diameter and adequate for work up to 4 in diameter, if the prongs are engaged deep enough. The tailstock centre can be either 'dead' or 'alive'. The dead ones are stationary points on which the wood rotates. There are two types: the conical for hard woods, the cup for soft woods. Both of these require some form of lubrication to prevent overheating and burning. Use a lubricant which is

Fig. 6.2 Finding the centre on the end of the wood for mounting between centres. Note the finger rubbing on the side to turn gauge

compatible with the finish to be used or waste the end $\frac{1}{2}$ in so that it is not part of the finished piece.

The live centres rotate on ball bearings and don't need any lubrication between them and the wood. They can also be tightened up much more. The live centre is almost essential for spindle turning and well worth the money.

Preparing the piece of wood to be held consists of:

1. Squaring the ends to give even contact with the prongs and a flat surface for the tail centre to penetrate.
2. Finding the centre. I usually do this by using the hand as a gauge, holding the pencil between thumb and first and second fingers while the third finger acts as a stop on the side of the wood. Than I guess the setting and draw a line from each side to give a small square on the end. The centre is in the middle. This works well on almost any shape of wood. Make a small location hole in the centre on each end.
3. If it is soft wood and less than $1\frac{1}{2}$ in diameter, it can be put between the centre points, and the prongs engaged by tightening up on the tailstock. Over $1\frac{1}{2}$ in and on hard woods, it is a good idea to make saw cuts on the drive end for the prongs, around $\frac{1}{8}$ in deep. This will give positive drive.
4. Tighten up the tailstock and you are ready to go. The dead centres will need adjusting as the turning progresses.

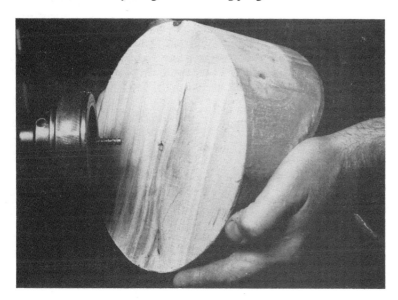

Fig. 6.3 Single screw chuck to hold bowl blank

Face plate

This is a flat round plate, which fits on to the headstock drive, with holes for screws to hold the wood. As a rough guide I would use a face plate which is between a quarter and one-third the diameter of the bowl up to 4 in thick. Screw penetration of $^3/_8$ in is adequate for most situations although $^1/_2$ in is necessary for heavy work. With light pieces, $^1/_4$ in might be enough. The surface of the wood must be flat for the wood to be rigid.

A single screw chuck is a good companion to the face plate. It can hold most pieces where the base is to be left 1 in thick or more, or it can hold a bowl on the top while the outside and the base are turned before mounting on the face plate. It can be made very easily with a face plate, a piece of 1 in ply and a coach bolt. It is one of the most useful holding devices on the lathe.

Of course, you will need to buy more chucks at some stage, but make sure that you are buying a solution to an existing problem and not one that you might have in the future.

STARTING TO TURN

Approaching the lathe with the first piece of wood is very exciting, and causes great apprehension. 'How do I hold the wood, how do I hold the tool, it is shaped and sharpened correctly, where do I stand?' All the answers should be there in your head and hands. The only unanswered question should be, 'what shall I make?' and that is the easiest one of all: 'Woodshavings' and lots of them. There are enough problems to face without creating unnecessary inhibitions about making mistakes and wasting a good piece of wood, changing from one tool to another in a vain attempt to produce a masterpiece at the first attempt.

Almost any piece of wood will do, about $2-2\frac{1}{2}$ in square or diameter and 12 in long, (or 1–2 in shorter than the toolrest: tree branches, offcuts from the local woodyard, hard wood, soft wood, pieces of old furniture, anything you can find avoiding knots and nails if possible. Two-by-two soft wood is ideal. If you are feeling very affluent then try some straight grained sycamore or beech. Not just one piece but 20 at least, or better 200, enough to spend time with each tool to become confident and familiar with their capabilities and limitations. It won't be easy at first but keep going and suddenly after a few days with the first tool everything will begin to fall into place. There is a great sense of achievement when you can control the tool to give a good smooth clean surface.

Only after mastering one tool is it wise to pick up a second and start again. This time the control and understanding will come much quicker as there are so many similarities between the tools. Again, only progress to further tools when fully confident with the previous one.

Once the wood is rotating the approach with the tool has to be firm and confident. Establish your position as master, hesitations create poor surfaces and occasionally the wood will wait its chance and bite back, usually with a bang as the tool digs in. Talk to yourself, describe what you are doing, how the tool is cutting, how you are standing, how you are holding the tool, then if you get a dig-in you will know precisely what you were doing the moment before to cause it. Fault analysis is important and this way you become your own black box recorder. Conversely if everything goes right then you will be able to repeat it.

Preparation

Each cut is made up of three directly connected movements, entry, cut and exit, which form the basis of the tool movement throughout the operation:

1. Entry, the initial contact between the wood and the cutting edge. This could be from a point if there is no bevel contact, as in making chamfers and 'V's. Or from a position of bevel contact as when rounding corners or making beads.
2. The cut. The object of the exercise during which the tool follows a predetermined path to shape the wood during which the shear angle is altered to suit the direction of cut at any particular point.
3. Exit. The end of the cut, where the cutting stops. This could be either a run off as at the end of a piece of wood and the tool retains the same angle as the cut as it runs off, or in a blind corner as at the bottom of a 'V', where the shear angle is increased to 90° for a clean finish.

For successful turning, each of these movements should be considered separately but should flow from one to the other as if they were one movement.

Deep fluted gouge

There is another decision to make. Which tool to start with? It does not really matter, as long as it is a gouge or chisel. My preference would be the ½ in deep fluted gouge or the ⅜ in as these would give

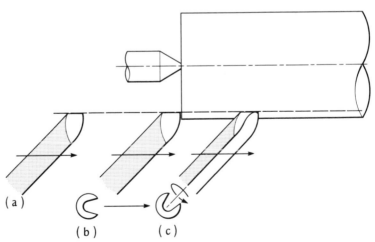

(a) Line up bevel for direction and depth of cut
(b) Make contact with wood on tip of tool first
(c) Once entry is made and bevel contact established. Tool can be twisted to angle for continuance of cut.

Fig. 7.1 Making an entry

confidence and quick results, establishing the principles of tool use over a wide range of cuts while minimising the risk of disastrous problems. If you don't have either of those then the $\frac{1}{2}$ in shallow fluted gouge can be subsituted, this will do the job as well but the depth of the cuts will have to be smaller. It also might be a good idea to use a smaller section of wood, say $1\frac{1}{2}$ in square. In any case these exercises should be repeated with the shallow fluted gouge after the deep fluted gouge.

For these exercises to work, the gouge should be shaped similar to the ones shown in Chapter 2. Other forms of grind may require a modified technique.

Fit the first piece of wood between centres, set the speed around 1500–1600 rpm, bring up the tool rest and set it as close as possible to the wood with the overhanging length at the tailstock end. The lathe is now ready. If you are a little nervous the speed could be set around 900–1200 rpm, but increase it as soon as possible.

Stand next to the tailstock, looking along the wood, hip against the bed, feet apart with the right foot slightly in front. Take the end of the tool handle in the left hand (control hand) with the tip on the overhang of the tool rest, twist the tool to the 80–90° shear cut position at the tip and point the bevel parallel to the lathe bed towards the headstock. Put the right hand (steady hand) underneath the tool with the index finger against the rest. (We need the stability to make the entry into the wood.) Hold the tool between the fingers and thumb. Check the position of the bevel relative to the outside of the wood to see how deep the cut will be. At first set it to miss the wood for a practice run. From standing in the start position move forward with tool as if cutting, to the finish position at the end of the piece of wood and check that the bevel is still parallel to the bed. Repeat this movement a number of times till you feel comfortable with it.

Now we are ready to try a cut. Stand out of the line of the wood and switch on. Don't worry about the noise, the corners flying round or any slight off centre in the wood as it will only take a few minutes with the gouge to sort it out. Take up the same position as for the practice run but with the tool set to give a $\frac{1}{4}$ in deep cut.

When ready, push both hands slowly but firmly forward at the same rate, taking care to keep the bevel parallel to the bed until the tool makes an entry into the wood and the bevel is rubbing behind the cutting edge. Even if it's only $\frac{1}{8}$ in or less, the control now comes to the left hand and the right is there for stability only.

Twist the tool back to between 60° and 70° shear, and continue the cutting by pushing along the tool with the left hand, moving the handle along at the same rate as the tip is moving, i.e. keeping the bevel parallel to the bed. The right hand should now be moved away from the rest and provide stability only by pulling the tool down onto the rest, the hand moving along with the tool and not the tool with the hand. Keep going, don't stop for anything. There is time to watch the cut as we move along. As the end of the cut is approaching, slow down the rate of feed, *not* by reducing pressure with the left hand but by pulling down harder with the right, almost like a tug of war between hands, and run through the end of the wood gently or splin-

Fig 7.2 Preparing to make an entry at the start of a long cut; tool rest overhang at the end where the cut starts; bevel lined up with direction of the cut; depth of cut set; gouge shear angle set near 90 degrees; fingers resting firmly on the tool rest for steady control on entry

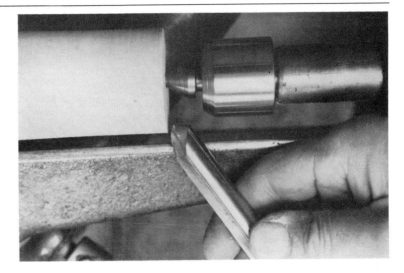

ters will fly. Don't stop the machine, return to the start position quickly and begin another cut exactly as before and keep going till the wood is down to ³/₄ in diameter.

Now you can stop the machine, admire the shavings on the floor and throw away the turned spindle. The next problem is recognising when the tool requires sharpening, this is more difficult when learning because if it isn't cutting well you may think you are doing something wrong and push a little harder. To avoid this situation sharpen the gouge for each of these practice pieces of wood. This will also be good sharpening practice.

Continue with more pieces and make each cut as if it is the final one, sorting out all the problems so that when the final cut does come you will be in automatic and it will just happen without thinking.

Fig. 7.3 The entry has been made and control is transferred from the finger on the tool rest to the bevel contact on the wood. The cut progressing, with the gouge shear reduced to around 60 degrees, fingers away from the rest and full control on the bevel

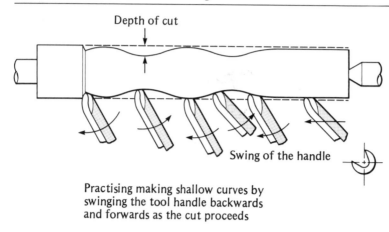

Fig. 7.4 Making shallow curves

Depth of cut

Swing of the handle

Practising making shallow curves by
swinging the tool handle backwards
and forwards as the cut proceeds

Once you are feeling confident and the piece in the lathe is round,
try gradually reducing the pressure from the steady hand during the
cut to the point where it is nonexistent and the hand can be taken
away. Now you will really feel that all the control is in the hand
holding the handle. That is why it is called 'the control hand', and it
could be either left or right. The idea behind practising with one
hand is to practically demonstrate the separate the functions of each
hand so that they can be kept separate. If the tool starts to chatter,
then the other hand can be brought back to steady it. This is the
steady hand. Remember that both hands are essential for the entry
and it is safer to use both throughout the cut. What you should have
produced is a series of long parallel flat surfaces. Now let's try a few
curves. Remember *all* the control is in the 'control hand'. The direction of cut is dictated by the direction the bevel is facing and the
pivoting point is the contact between the wood and the bevel. To
change the direction of cut we must change the direction of the bevel
by swinging the handle in the control hand, pivoting the tool at the
bevel.

First rough down the next piece to the round and start a cut in the
normal way, as you move along, gradually swing the handle forward
a few inches and the tool will move into the wood. When it has gone
in a further $\frac{1}{4}$ in swing the handle backwards to bring it out again,
then return it to the parallel cutting position.

Repeat this a number of times along the length of the wood.

When you feel confident, try making the cut single handed,
keeping the pressure constant and you will really begin to understand about handling the tools. We are not necessarily cutting the
wood the way it prefers to be cut but demonstrating form and tool
control, building skill and confidence ready for future projects.

Squaring ends

Squaring the ends is next, which means we want to make a cut at
right angles to the centre line of the lathe. Start with a rounded piece

Fig. 7.5 Square shoulders and chamfers with the gouge

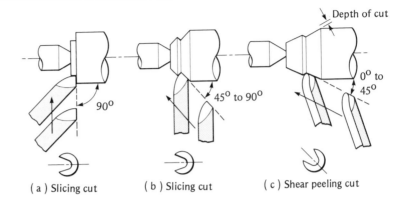

(a) Slicing cut   (b) Slicing cut   (c) Shear peeling cut

of wood, and work at the tailstock end. This type of cut is really a 'detail' cut. All the action is localised without much movement along the rest and the cut often approaches the axis. For this it is a good idea to lower the rest so that the centre of the tool is at lathe axis height or just above. This avoids having to raise the handle above the horizontal when approaching the centre. It is also a good idea to hold the gouge underhand with the index finger fixed firmly against the rest, allowing the tool to slide through the fingers to complete the cut. The steady hand should hold the bevel firmly against the wood. Set the gouge to the 85–90° shear for a slicing cut, point the bevel in the direction of travel, positioned to take a $\frac{1}{16}$ in cut and stand looking down the bevel. The right hand will now be the control hand and the left the support hand. The tip in this situation will be making a slicing cut while the lower part of the flute will scrape. The entry is made just as before, but the tool is kept in the 85–90° shear position while running down the face for what is a good clean slicing cut of the end grain, pushing with the control hand, steadying with the steady hand. Stop at $\frac{3}{4}$ in diameter minimum or just before the tailstock centre is reached (whichever comes first) and repeat the cut as many times as possible.

Chamfers

The procedure for a chamfer depends on the angle to the axis, from 0–45° the type of cut being made by the tip is a shear peeling cut, from 45–90° to the axis the type of cut taken by the tool tip is a slicing cut. Try both of them.

First a 60° chamfer. The procedure is the same as for squaring the end. Place the tool on the rest with bevel set at 60° to the axis and the shear at 85–90° ready to make the entry and take a $\frac{1}{16}$ in deep cut at the tailstock end. Stand behind the bevel and make the entry as for squaring the end. The shear angle is left at 85–90° throughout for a slicing cut.

Now try these cuts at the headstock end. There will be a difference because we will be back to holding the tool exactly as we were when running along the wood, left hand control, right hand steady. The procedure will be exactly the same as at the opposite end.

To make a shallower chamfer, say 30°, the cut at the tip is shear peeling. Because the entry is shallow the tip will automatically make first contact followed by bevel support, therefore the tool can be set at the angle for the remainder of the cut, in this case about 60° shear.

As before, line up the bevel, set the shear angle, take a firm position with the support hand on the tool rest, then move the tool forward and make the entry. Continue the move to the end of the cut. If there is any problem on entry with any of these cuts, first check that you are setting up the tool correctly, and are holding it firmly, and try again. If the problem still persists, make a dummy entry with the lathe stopped and check that the first contact is made at the tip of the tool immediately followed by bevel support. Adjust the shear angle if necessary to obtain the correct contact.

'V' cuts

We are still using the deep fluted gouge but it might be a good idea to use a smaller one for these detail cuts, say $\frac{1}{4}$ in or $\frac{3}{8}$ in, but the $\frac{1}{2}$ in

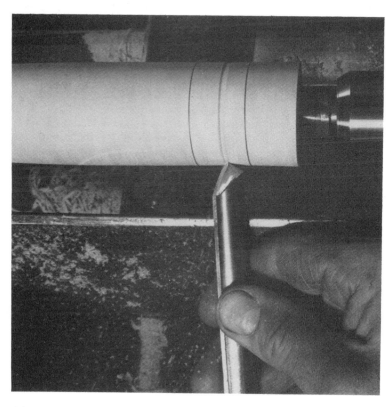

Fig. 7.6 Starting to cut a shallow 'V' with the deep fluted gouge

Fig. 7.7 Final cut of the 'V'. Note the direction of the bevel

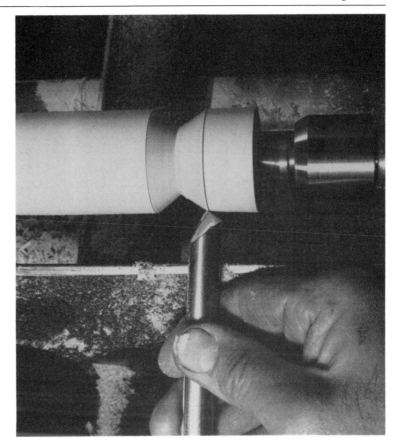

will do the job just as well. The profile of the tool will determine the minimum angle of the 'V'. In this case, the tool angle is just under 90° so let's make the 'V' at 100° to give us some working space. It is more a matter of judging by eye than measuring, which gets easier with practice. We have already made the type of cut we want in the chamfer on the ends, but this time they are face to face, two 40° chamfers, (less than 45°, therefore a shear peeling cut). Put on two pencil lines which will represent the boundaries. Because we are going to be making alternate cuts on opposite faces of the 'V' then we need to stand in one position to avoid unnecessary movement. There are two positions to consider, the first is standing square onto the wood in the line with the centre of the 'V' but with feet wide apart (about 18 in) so that we can sway from one side to another to be in the correct position for each cut without moving our feet. The tool will change hands for each side. The second is to stand slightly to one side in a position to look vertically down on the 'V' and this time the tool stays in the same hand all the time. The second method is much more economical in both time and movement. Try both positions to see which you prefer. I use both, so it must depend on the mood I'm in.

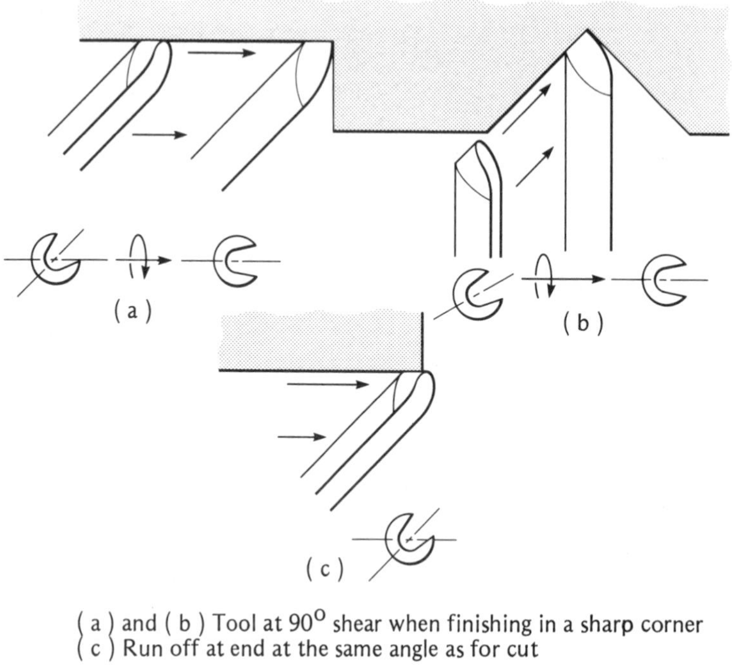

Fig. 7.8 Finishing cut

(a) and (b) Tool at 90° shear when finishing in a sharp corner
(c) Run off at end at the same angle as for cut

Fig. 7.9 Making a square shoulder. First remove the waste up to the shoulder, two or three cuts should be enough

Place the tool on the rest with about 70° shear, set the bevel to give the required angle with the tip just to one side of the centre and make a small cut about ⅛ in deep as the tool approaches the bottom of the 'V'. Twist the tool to the 90° shear position for a sharp finish. The width of the cut will increase as the tool goes in because there is no clearance. Make the second cut in exactly the same way on the other side of the 'V'.

The rest is just a matter of repeating this sequence until the lines on either side are reached. Finish all the cuts 90° shear and the result will be a crisp and clean 'V'.

Square shoulders

Making a square shoulder is just the same as squaring the ends but working further along the piece. Reduce the diameter, at the tail-stock end, of the first two inches to 1 in by running in from the end and stopping, two or three runs should do it. With the tool end close to being square at the end, the shoulder is almost made and just needs cleaning up. If you are turning soft wood, then there is a risk of the corners splintering off ahead of the tool and beyond the point of the shoulder. To avoid this it is better to make a 'V' cut just before the shoulder, then remove the waste up to that first. To square the shoulder, set the tool on the rest at 85–90° shear for a slicing cut, the

Fig. 7.10 Squaring the shoulder with the tip slicing and the bottom edge scraping. Note the line of the bevel. The fact that the stock is square makes no difference

bevel square to the lathe and make the cut as for squaring the ends. Don't forget to stand looking down the bevel. Take a lot of these cuts to get the feel of the position and movement then repeat at the other end where the left hand becomes the controlling hand. Finish the corner by taking a final cut along the wood into the corner.

Fig. 7.11 Finish cut in high shear for a clean corner

Fig. 7.12 Putting a chamfer on a square stock, the same procedure as for round stock

Square stock

We have been doing these cuts on a round stock. They are performed in exactly the same way when the stock is still square but it just needs a little more care and confidence when entering the wood, keeping fingers well clear of the square corners. Put a piece of 2 in × 2 in between the centres and switch on. There is an obvious sight difficulty because the edges of the wood are less clearly defined when it is rotating. It is more of a problem when doing detailed work, rather than roughing out, but can be minimised by adjusting lighting and

Fig. 7.13 Shoulder rounded with deep fluted gouge

line of sight. Now square up both ends as before, the tool is held and the entry made as if it were a solid round piece. In fact, the speed at which it is rotating gives the illusion of roundness and for all practical purposes it is round. Once the ends have been squared off, try a 45° chamfer. Once again the approach is as for round wood. Set the bevel and the shear, stand looking down the bevel, make sure that the steady hand is firmly against the rest, then make the cut. The chamfer on the square wood produces interesting shapes between the flat and round surfaces which can be incorporated into designs later on.

The 'V' cut is exactly the same as before, the approach has to be firm and positive to maintain control. Try 'V' cuts at different angles until the whole piece is covered with them and note the patterns obtained.

The cove

The cove is the next form which fits into this group, because the method of entry is the same as for squaring the ends. First consider the shape: it is a semi circle the ends of which are square to the axis and the rest is circular with a diameter the same as the width across the top. It needs to be tight and sharp to look right. The shape itself tells us how the tool entry is made. It is square to the axis just the same as for making a square shoulder or squaring the end of the piece. Entry is made with the bevel square to the lathe axis. The cutting edge is at 90° shear and because there are two sides as in a 'V' cut, there will be two entries, one from either side which will meet in the middle.

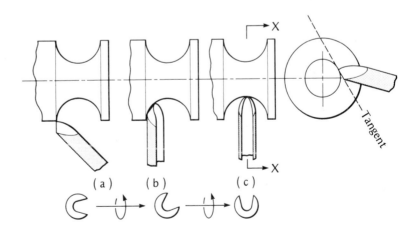

(a) Start position as for slicing cut
(b) Part way round the cove as the handle is swung round and the tool is twisted
(c) Finished position with the tip taking a peeling cut with zero shear to allow the tool to fit into the cove

Fig. 7.14 Cutting a cove

We can't just swing the tool round in the 90° shear position because there is not enough room to get the bevel and cutting edge flat in the bottom of the cove. For this, the tool needs to end up square to the lathe axis in almost the 0° shear position, with the bevel rubbing beneath the cutting edge. The tool movement from start to finish of the cut is a combination of twist and swing. Before starting the machine, try the motion required. Press the steady hand against the tool rest and hold the tool in the tips of the finger and thumb underhand. The control hand should also hold the handle in the tips of fingers and thumb so as to be able to twist the tool. Because there are cuts on both sides of the cove, stand to one side (as when making the 'V') so that it can be completed without changing hands. First put the tool in the start position, 90° shear and the bevel square to the axis, then twist and swing the tool round to the finish position. When you are happy and comfortable with the movement, try doing the cut. As with the 'V', take cuts from alternate sides, working outwards, until the final shape is complete. Practise with lots of coves until you are happy with the results and you will probably find that the cove can be made with only one or two cuts from each side. It might also be a good idea to practice making half coves to start with, at the ends of the wood. Big tools make big coves, the width of the tool should not be more than about half the width of the cove and the radius on the end of the gouge less than the radius of the cove, and preferably not more than half. This is the sort of situation where the shape to which the tool is ground is important for access.

A change of entry

All our entries into the wood up to now have had one thing in common, the cutting edge has entered, followed by the bevel from a

Fig. 7.15 Making entry along the piece

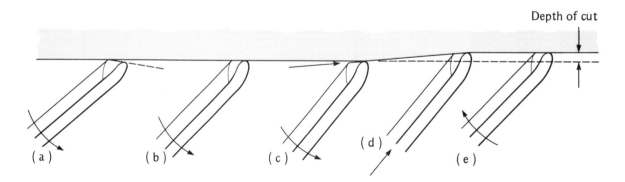

Depth of cut

(a) First contact of tool to wood with the heel of the bevel
(b) Handle swung forward pivoting on bevel to bring full bevel contact
(c) Handle swung further forward to bring cutting edge into contact with the wood
(d) Push along handle for tool to enter wood and make cut
(e) Handle swung back to bring bevel parallel to original surface for constant depth of cut

point of no contact with wood. This always applies where there is a sharp change in direction as in the case of 'V's, chamfers and square shoulders etc.

For other shapes and forms, i.e. large convex and concave curves, beads and round shoulders, another type of entry is appropriate.

Starting the cut part of the way along the piece from where the curve is blended in with the existing surface, there is bevel contact before entry. To make this entry, place the tool on the rest and set the tip to the approximate cutting angle. Make contact with the heal of the bevel first (which should be rubbing behind the cutting edge), gradually swing the handle forward until full bevel contact is made. To begin the cut, swing the handle further forward at the same time pushing along the handle to feed the cut. Once entry is complete, the handle can be swung either backwards or forwards to continue the cut in the required direction.

Large convex to concave curves

In a way we have already done large curves when learning control of the tool, swinging the handle backwards and forwards to make the tool go in and out of the wood. In this exercise we want to make an entry along the wood, then follow a specific shape: a large convex curve followed by a concave curve. The wood should be turned round first for initial practice.

The start position is as for the entry above, with the tool set in the rest, bevel against the wood parallel to the axis with 45–70° shear as if it were making a cut along the surface. Because the angles of these curves are to be shallow, there is no need to alter the shear angle of the tool as the cut proceeds. Start near the end of the wood and gradually work back to the final shape with subsequent cuts. Make each cut as if it were the last one, following the final shape right from the start. Stand behind the bevel, hold the tool onto the rest with the support hand, then with the control hand, push along the tool and at the same time swing the handle slowly forward and the tool will enter the wood, making a convex curve. The concave section is achieved by maintaining the push on the handle and swinging the handle slowly backwards to a position where the bevel is parallel to the axis. Repeat the exercise with the same shape at the opposite end.

You may notice, if you try a very sharp concave curve, that the radius will be limited by the length of the bevel on the tool. Choose a size of curve to match the tool. Working on square stock, the procedure is identical and should be tried at this stage.

Beads and round corners

A round corner is an arc of 90° from a line parallel to the axis to a line square to the axis. Beads come in two types, the first is a proud bead which sits nicely on top of the spindle. It's a mirror image of a cove.

The second type of bead is an inset one and is dependant on the profile of the tool being used as to the angle in the corner.

As the cuts taken in making round corners and bead are fairly light, fluidity and firmness of control are very important. The handle moves a long way while the cutting edge moves only a very short distance, creating a tendency for the tip to run ahead out of control. The steady hand can help by holding the tool back by pressing it firmly onto the wood resulting in both hands acting against each other, the control hand should be allowed to win to obtain a smooth, controlled cut.

There are two ways of making corners and proud beads: The first is to start with the tool horizontal in a high shear cut position and the bevel parallel to the axis. To make the cut, swing the handle round almost 90° until the bevel is square to the axis. At the same time, twist the tool slightly to bring it 90° shear for the slicing cut. The control hand can grip the handle with the full hand throughout the movement as there is little twist. The steady hand is held firm against the rest, holding the tool underhand with fingers only to allow it to slide through them as the cut proceeds.

This method is ideal for large corners and beads. Plenty of room is needed to swing the handle. The second is to start with very low angle of shear, the bevel rubbing below the cutting edge, from where the tool is both twisted to 90° shear and swung round until the bevel is square to the axis to complete the curve.

The control hand holds the handle in the fingers in order to twist the tool. The steady hand is firmly anchored to the rest, with the index finger hooked underneath it and holding the tool with fingertips pressing it onto the rest and the wood, allowing the tool to twist in the fingers.

This is a more compact movement requiring less swing of the handle, ideal for average and small detail work where fine control is needed. The finish position is identical in both cases, bevel square to the axis and at 90° shear.

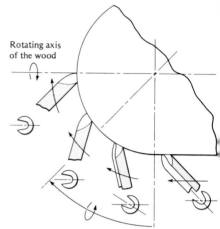

Rotating axis of the wood

Area over which the tool is twisted as the cutting action changes from shear peeling to slicing

Working round a curve changing from a shear peeling cut to a slicing cut

Fig. 7.16 Rotation of tool round a curve

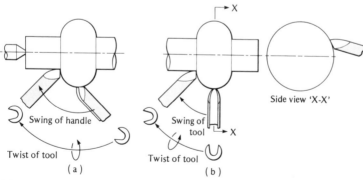

Swing of handle

Twist of tool

(a)

X

Swing of tool

X

Twist of tool

(b)

Side view 'X-X'

(a) Start position: High shear angle
Tool movement: Large swing of handle with small twist of the tool.
Suitable for large beads.

(b) Start position: Very low shear angle.
Tool movement: Small swing of handle with large twist of the tool.
Suitable for small beads requiring fine control.

Fig. 7.17 Turning beads with the gouge

Fig 7.18 Making a bead with the deep fluted gouge

Try both of these methods of rounding corners, but first do some dummy runs. Stand in the start position then swing the handle round first to the 45° position and check that the shear angle is 90°, then onto the finish position. When you are happy with the movement, try the cuts.

Inset beads

Probably the best way to make this bead is to cut the 'V' first then round the corners as described above.

The shape of an inset bead is determined to some extent by the profile of the tool used to cut it. Using the deep fluted gouge is very limiting because its access is restricted. To start the bead, cut two 'V's with the same tool to be used for the beads (then we are sure that it will fit into the 'V'). Follow the second method of cutting the beads described above. The only difference being that the finish position for the cut is when the bevel is in line with the 'V'.

What other cuts do we need for this kind of work? Only parting off, or to be able to make tighter Vs and beads. That can't be bad for one tool which is often referred to as a 'bowl turner'.

What you will have found with this tool is that it creates very few problems, and it will cut however it is presented to the wood. Just because it is cutting, don't assume that the cut is being made right. Check what it is doing to get the best out of it.

Summary

From this one tool we have learned most of what there is to know about the tools, how they work and how to use then, so it's worth going over the main points again.

1. Approach the wood with the tool in a firm, positive manner to establish your position as master.
2. Stand behind the bevel looking in the direction of travel whenever possible.
3. Hold the gouge in the horizontal position or just a few degrees below.
4. Set the angle of shear for the particular cut.
5. The hand holding the handle is the control hand and should push along the handle.
6. The other hand is a steady hand and should not push or pull, but only press the tool onto the rest or wood.
7. The direction of cut is the direction the bevel is pointing.
8. Directional control is obtained by swinging the handle, pivoting on the bevel to change the direction it is pointing.

Bowl turning

It may seem strange that all the practice with the 'bowl turning' gouge has been on spindle work, but if you can use it there then you can use it on bowls without any problems. All the same rules apply relating to slicing and shear peeling but remember that to 'cut the wood as it prefers to be cut' the directions the tools should face are reversed. Face from small to large diameter on the outside and from large to small diameter on the inside.

The way to start is with scrap wood; 'green' wood is ideal.

Mount a round blank, 6–8 in diameter, 3 in thick, on a face plate or single screw ready for turning. Set the lathe speed around 90 rpm.

Practise making the outside shape of a bowl, starting at the base and working to the rim. The cuts, right from the first one, should follow the final shape. Place the tool rest at centre line height square across the base, put the gouge on the rest, pointing the bevel in the direction of cut. Stand looking down the bevel and hold the gouge at about 60° shear set for a cut about $\frac{1}{4}$ in deep. Plan a very simple shape of bowl, straight sided 'V' shape for easy turning. The entry as before has to be firm and positive, once this is made then all the con-

Fig. 7.19 Turning the outside of the bowl

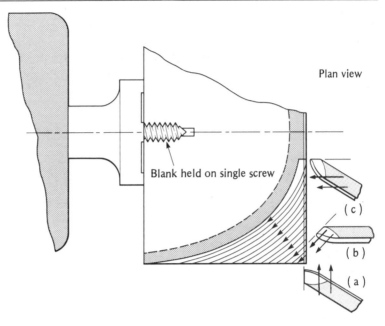

Plan view

Blank held on single screw

(c)

(b)

(a)

The only real important cut is the last one which
should be a long sweep.
To achieve this without problems, start by following
the final shape from the first cut, gradually refining
the shape and achieving the surface finish required.
When the last cut comes it will be almost automatic
and without problems.
(a) First cut to clean up base, making subsequent entries easier.
(b) Roughing and finishing cuts.
(c) Cutting spigot for chuck

trol is in the control hand, the steady hand just holds the tool on the
rest. The cut and directional control are exactly as practised on
spindle work. Wood will be removed very qickly, increasing the tool
overhang. Before it gets to 2 in move the tool rest in line with the
turned surface. The aim is to make the cuts from base to rim in one
movement for a smooth final shape. Remember to keep the tool held
firmly against the wood for stability and control.

You should soon be confident enough to reduce the support from
the support hand to feel the true control in the control hand.

The base needs to be flattened. For this, the cut is a slicing cut
from outside to centre. Set the tool rest parallel to the base so that
the centre of the tool is at lathe centre line height. Point the bevel at
90° to the axis and set at 85° shear, stand looking down the bevel
ready to make a $\frac{1}{8}$ in deep cut. Make the entry as before, keeping the
bevel exactly on 90° to the axis all the way down for a flat base. *Do
not* use the rest as a guide. Slow down as you get near to the centre to
carefully remove the pip. This should be gently sliced off with the tip
off the tool.

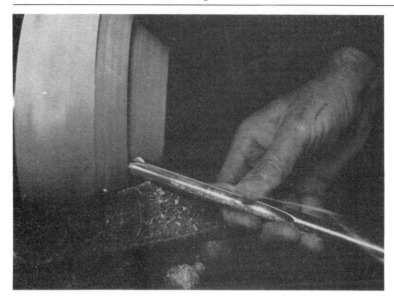

Fig. 7.20 Shaping up the outside of a bowl blank, working from the base to the rim, following the final shape right from the first cut

A spigot can be made on the base by making the same cut but this time the bevel is parallel to the axis and at 90° shear for the entry up to the shoulder. Everything is exactly the same as for the cuts we made parallel to the axis into a corner on the spindle.

That should cover all the cuts on the outside of a simple bowl

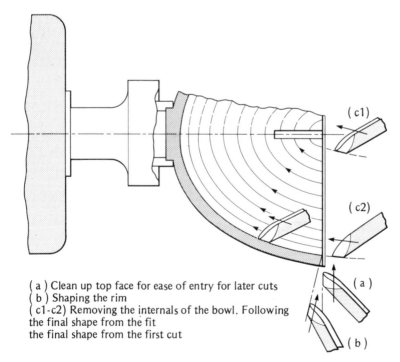

(a) Clean up top face for ease of entry for later cuts
(b) Shaping the rim
(c1-c2) Removing the internals of the bowl. Following
the final shape from the fit
the final shape from the first cut

Fig. 7.21 Turning the inside of a bowl

Fig. 7.22 Turning out the inside, working from the rim to the base, following outside shape from the first cut

which you should practise until completely confident. The product should be bags of wood shavings.

The inside is next. For this, turn an outside bowl shape as above and mount it on a 3 in face plate. Make the first cut across the top, which is the same as flattening the base on the outside. This isn't essential but it is good practice and will make the entries easier when hollowing out.

The next part of the bowl to turn is the rim, as it is more difficult and risky when you are down to the final thickness. Make the rim square to the outside so that we can see precisely how thick the rim is. This also looks good from a design point of view. The cut can be made either way, centre to outside or outside to centre. Often there is little difference. Stand looking down the bevel, be firm and give plenty of support from the support hand, with a high shear angle. Make a few very light cuts until the rim is $1\frac{1}{2}$ in wide. If the edges left are very sharp, then round them ever so slightly with the tool or a fine sand paper. This is just a safety precaution to avoid cutting the hand later on.

Now we are ready to start hollowing out. Always start in the centre and work outwards. Follow the outside shape right from the very first cut so that at all stages the thickness of the bowl is even. Sort out all the problems on the early cuts and the finish cuts will come automatically.

Set the gouge on the rest, shear angle around 75°, bevel parallel with the outside at the rim. Stand looking down the bevel ready to make the cut. The entry can cause problems sometimes with the tip of the tool skidding along the surface making a spiral groove right to the rim. Don't try solving the problem by artificial means, such as making grooves with the scraper to prevent the run. Sort out the root cause and do the cut right. The most likely causes are: not being firm

Fig. 7.23 As the thickness reduces, the wall requires support, the fingers of the control hand around the outside while the thumb supports the tool

enough in approach or inadequate support from the control hand which should be pressed firmly against the rest, or tool presentation wrong with the initial cut not being followed immediately by bevel support. Adjust the shear angle at contact and make shallower cuts and that should solve it. If there is still a problem, it could be that the profile of the tip is wrong and requires reshaping. For any problem in turning, sort out the cause and put it right. Remember, two wrongs don't make a right.

As this is the inside of a bowl, the tool tip goes down the side then across the bottom. This means that the handle will be swung out-wards towards the body, so allow some clearance between body and tool at the start of the cuts.

Set the gouge to take a $\frac{1}{4}$ in wide cut from the centre then make a firm entry and swing the handle backwards to bring the tip square to the axis at the centre. No matter how small a cut that was, it should be bowl-shaped and a pattern for all the subsequent cuts to follow.

As the cuts get longer we can look at the shear angle as the tool moves from rim to base. At entry the shear angle is fairly high, if there are any problems at this point the shear should be increased to almost 90° and if they persist reduce the depth of cut because the problem probably lies in the shape and sharpness of the cutting edge.

Once the entry is made the shear should be reduced to around 70° on the roughing cut, as the tool comes across the base. Then the shear should be increased to near 90° for a slicing cut up to the pip.

When the rim is 2 in wide, stop the lathe and feel the thickness all the way down. If it isn't even, make adjustments to the path of the tool at this stage. Do the same at 1 in thick.

By this time you will have removed quite a lot of wood and the tool won't be as sharp as it was to start with. This is the time to re-sharpen because we want to make the remaining cuts consecutively so that we are in automatic and the final cut comes out without thinking. For the last cut the shear angle can be increased to improve the finish.

As the bowl gets thinner then it will probably need additional support to stop bending or vibration. This is where the steady hand plays a dual role. The fingers are positioned on the outside of the bowl to support the wood directly behind the tool, while the thumb supports the tool on entry.

With any luck, the bowl should be smooth and an even thickness all the way down.

If you leave the thickness around $\frac{3}{4}$ in then there is plenty of wood left to practise, evening the surface with the scraper if necessary.

As with all the other exercises, make plenty of wood shavings before trying a finished bowl.

Shallow fluted gouge

The shallow fluted gouge is, as it says, a gouge with a shallow flute. Other names by which it is often known are, spindle gouge or detail gouge, but this last name may only apply to the smaller end of the range.

Shallow fluted gouges are made in two ways, up to $\frac{3}{8}$ in the stock is round bar, $\frac{1}{2}$ in and above the tool has a forged form. In fact it is unreasonable to lump them together in the same range because the handling and cutting characteristics are very different, with the different stocks and shapes of flutes.

Forged forms

The forged gouges are very much like slightly bent chisels, being used mostly for long shear pealing and slicing cuts with minimal, if any, scraping cut. The balance of the tool and the handling characteristics are also similar to the chisel because, in certain attitudes, the support on the tool rest is not in line with the cutting forces, creating a turning moment on the gouge and causing it to rely on the bevel for support.

The big difference is that it is only sharpened on one side and that is usually in a curve.

Round stock

Even within the three round stock gouges there are differences, the $\frac{1}{2}$ in and $\frac{3}{8}$ in have a flute radius of $\frac{1}{4}$ in giving them different profiles. They are not scaled versions of the same shape. The $\frac{1}{4}$ in gouge on the other hand has a 0.094 in radius flute, making it much more like a deep fluted gouge in section. I would be quite happy if it were called a deep fluted gouge, sharpened and used as such.

In use, there are obvious similarities in cutting actions and the round section shallow fluted gouge could carry out all the operations practised on the deep fluted gouge. Indeed these should be repeated as the practice for shallow fluted gouge. The differences will soon become apparent. The amount of scraping action will be reduced while the more rounded bottom to the flute will give greater length to the peeling action. This would mean that only shallower cuts are possible but there may be an improvement in the quality of the finish.

The choice of tool for any particular job is very much a personal preference as there is considerable overlap in what they can do. My choice of tool, where possible, is the deep fluted gouge which, as we have seen, will do almost everything, and certainly anything the shallow fluted gouge can do.

Roughing gouge

This is in a category of its own, and there are just two sizes in the range: $\frac{3}{4}$ in and $1\frac{1}{4}$ in. I have the $1\frac{1}{4}$ in. The width of the flute is $1\frac{1}{8}$ in and the overall width is $1\frac{1}{2}$ in. (so why call it $1\frac{1}{4}$ in?). The wall thickness is even at $\frac{5}{32}$ in all the way round, and the overall depth is $\frac{3}{4}$ in. The flute has an almost semicircular bottom running into straight sides, a hybrid which you might expect from crossing one of the forged shapes of shallow fluted gouge with a deep fluted gouge.

Mine is still ground much as it was when bought, square across the end and the bevel at 45°. Not that this is necessarily the best form, just that it has not had enough use to evolve to any other. The length of the cutting edge is aprox $1\frac{3}{4}$ in.

As the title suggests, the purpose of this tool is roughing down to a round section from any shape of blank, square being the most

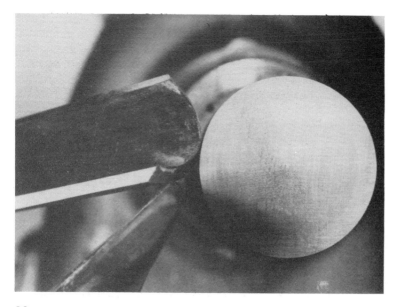

Fig. 7.24 Roughing gouge

Fig. 7.25 90 degrees shear with roughing gouge horizontal

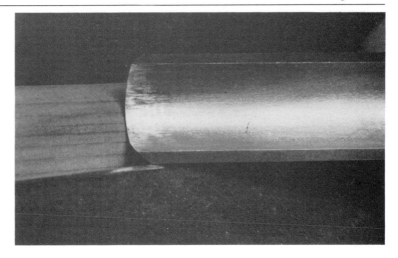

obvious one. It can also make long sweeping curves, leaving a good finish.

Using this shape of cutting edge gives the tool quite different characteristics to the type of grind on the deep fluted gouge. To demonstrate this, set up a 2 in diameter × 12 in long section between centres, and set the tool rest at ¹⁄₂ in below the axis. Place the gouge horizontally on the rest, pointing the bevel parallel along the axis and set so that the centre of the tool contacts the wood. I haven't specified the shear angle but it will be 90°. Looking around the edge to the bottom straight section we will see that it is in the scraping attitude. Now twist the tool 45°, keeping the contact bevel parallel and the tool horizontal. If we now look at the point of contact, the shear angle is still 90° and that the lowest part of the flute is in the scraping position just as before.

Fig. 7.26 Shear angle at point of contact is 60 degrees. (The handle is dropped approximately 30 degrees from 90 degrees to 60 degrees.) Note that twisting the roughing gouge does not alter the shear angle at point of contact

Twisting the gouge a further 45°, the shear angle at the point of contact is still 90° and the lowest part of the flute, which is now the centre, is in the scraping position.

From this we can see that just twisting the tool does not alter the cutting angles at all, but it does allow the whole of the cutting edge to be used in exactly the same way. Of course we know that a shear angle of 90° will not cut along the surface so we need to change it. Drop the handle down about 30°, maintaining the bevel contact. You will not only notice the change in the shear peel angle, but the lower edge of the flute will be in a peeling attitude and not scraping. Twisting the gouge in this position will maintain these cutting angles. So it is possible to use all of the cutting edge before regrinding. The control and stability are exactly the same as the deep fluted gouge, keeping the bevel rubbing and pressing it against the wood.

Because the end of the gouge is square across, the angle between the rough face and the finished face as made by the tool is 135°, making the angle of the cutting face to the direction of travel 45°, as compared with 90° on the deep fluted gouge shape. This sometimes reduces the directional control of the tool because there can be a tendency for it to pull out of the cut and slide along the rough face rather than the finish face, particularly when taking a fine cut. In that situation the support hand should hold the gouge onto the bevel as well as onto the rest. The length of the cutting edge for a given depth of cut is longer than for the deep fluted gouge. The downward force on the cutting edge is to the work side of the support point on the rest, which has tendency to twist the gouge towards the work piece. A firm hand grip is all that is necessary to resist it, and it's advisable to cut well away from the points to avoid a dig-in.

Making a cut with this tool is very simple. You will have already set it up in a cutting position in the previous demonstration. Now you have a choice as to whether you start along the piece and gradually swing the tool into the wood in exactly the same way as the deep

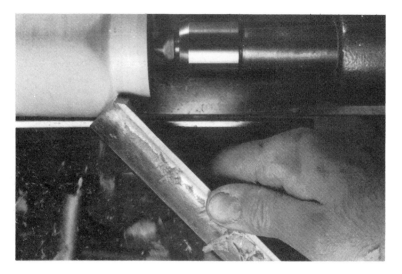

Fig. 7.27 Roughing from round to square in one operation with the roughing gouge. The direction of bevel and travel is from right to left

fluted gouge or the chisel. Alternatively, you can start right at the end. Set the gouge at the required cutting angles alongside the wood, slide it backwards, parallel to the axis, until it is clear of the wood then move it towards the axis by the depth of cut required. To start with, say between $\frac{1}{8}$in and $\frac{1}{4}$in, depending on how confident you feel. Now you are ready to switch on the machine. Entry is made with the tool in the same attitude as for the following cut, all that is required is that the gouge is pushed confidently forward. Once full bevel contact is made, the hand holding the handle takes control, with the other hand in support. You can run from one end of the piece to the other but, if you are turning square soft wood beware of possible splinters flying as you approach the last inch or so. Doing this will improve your confidence and make you aware of how the wood reacts because there are lots of situations where you have to run off the end. Drawing the tool back in exactly the same position will also take a cut, making roughing down a very fast operation.

Practise making long straight cuts first, as if you were making a rolling pin, then make long curves at the ends to get the feel of shape control. This is a very nice tool to use, being very fast and efficient at roughing down, taking cuts up to $\frac{1}{2}$in easily, as well as making short work of the corners. I imagine that the $\frac{3}{4}$in will also be very useful, particularly for smaller work, although I would hesitate at buying both of them as there would be very little to gain. It would be interesting to try shaping the gouge the same way as the deep fluted gouge to see how it performed. The $\frac{3}{4}$in would be the one to try for better access on fine detail.

By now you should be beginning to realise that there is very little difference in picking up and using any of the tools. When you can use and understand one tool, then the others are mastered very quickly.

Chisels

Chisels have two modes of operation. The first uses the long cutting edge, which can either peel or slice. The other uses the points of the chisel only. I am unable to find a name for this type of cutting in other woodturning books. There should be one, so for this book I will call it 'pointing'.

The most popular chisel is the straight skew. It has a deserved reputation as a very pernickety tool and if used incorrectly it takes sudden revenge by severely digging into the wood. The problem, and the solution, lie in the hands of the turner, who needs to understand the tool much more, although there is some room for improvement in the design.

It also has a reputation of being a very versatile tool, producing excellent finishes. This is very true, but saying that is partly to devalue the other tools undeservedly as some of them can match the chisel with minimal risk. The area in which the chisel is supreme is in access. The narrow flat tool with an acute cutting edge can fit into less than half the angle of any of the other cutting tools (not

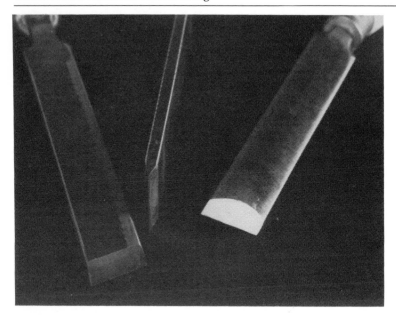

Fig. 7.28 Chisels

scrapers). The sort of access required to make narrow 'V's, beads and corners, essential elements in spindle turning.

I don't know why the manufacturers persist in making the chisel out of rectangular sections with very sharp corners, in particular the new HSS chisels. This is the biggest problem with the tool, it will not slide gently along the rest. It will catch on every little nick and if there are none there it will very quickly make its own. How often in this situation do we assume that we are doing something wrong, we try pushing harder then the tool jumps and digs in, or we think the chisel needs sharpening or it's bad bit of wood, when all the time it's the manufacturer, making a tool that looks good on the shelf and is useless on the lathe.

Take one of the new HSS chisels, place it horizontally on the rest with a shear angle of 45° and at 45° to the direction of travel, and put a little pressure downwards with the support hand. Don't switch on, or even put any wood in, try the movement along the rest to take a cut. If you manage to move $\frac{1}{2}$ in then you did very well. If you moved further then you were not putting on enough pressure with the support hand to simulate the normal use of the tool. The solution to this problem is to round off the corners (see diagram). Now try the slide test. There should be an amazing difference, and that little exercise should solve a major problem in using the chisel. It will also help if the surface of the tool rest is maintained flat and smooth..

That should help you sort out your existing chisels. Sorby have eliminated the problem for the future tools with their elliptical stock chisel, which sounds quite revolutionary but is really long overdue. I have tried the new chisel and found it to be light and very smooth in operation, although I am not quite sure that the small flat on the long edge is necessary.

Fig. 7.29 Chisels

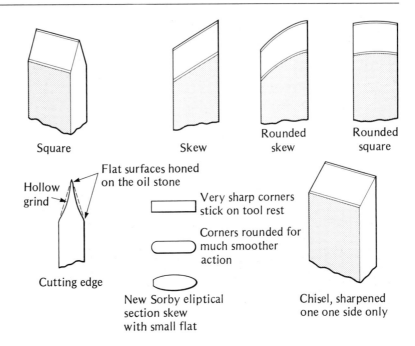

Square   Skew   Rounded skew   Rounded square

Flat surfaces honed on the oil stone

Hollow grind

Cutting edge

Very sharp corners stick on tool rest

Corners rounded for much smoother action

New Sorby eliptical section skew with small flat

Chisel, sharpened one one side only

To work at all, the chisel needs to be very sharp, otherwise excessive force will be necessary, creating many other problems. As with any tool, one of the biggest problems when learning is recognising when the problem is a blunt tool. The rule I use is 'when in doubt re-sharpen'. You will always have a sharp tool, and it is good practice for sharpening. This may cost up to $\frac{1}{4}$ in of the tool during your learning period but it is a small price to pay. As you become accustomed to the tools, then you may wish to reduce the frequency of grinding.

Peeling cuts

For a large section of its work, the chisel is used in the 'shear peeling' mode to make cuts parallel to the axis. The cutting edge is angled in such a way as to face the direction of travel and the rotating surface of the wood. The bevel is rubbing on the wood behind the cutting edge in the direction of travel, providing support for the tool and a control surface, as described in Chapter 3 and very similar to the tip action of the deep fluted gouge which we have just covered.

Select a piece of wood to practice on, red wood or pine, straight grained and without knots. Keep to a 'soft' wood as the cutting will be easier and the cutting edge will last longer. Also it's cheaper. Rough down a 12 in long, 2 in square section between centres to round using the roughing gouge.

If you have a choice of chisels, try the square ended chisel to start

Fig. 7.30 Shear peeling. Travel is from left to right

with, selecting one of a suitable size for use on 2 in work, a 1 in chisel should be OK, $\frac{3}{4}$ in could be on the small side, $1\frac{1}{4}$ in though large, would be better. If you don't have a square one, it is not essential, use a skewed chisel but read on a little further to find out which way to use it.

The height of the rest needs to be set, remembering that while the stock has an initial diameter of 2 in it is going to be reduced and could come down to 1 in or less. A good height at which to start is for the top of the rest to be at the centre line height (or at least $\frac{1}{4}$ in below the top of the smallest finished diameter of the wood).

Start by placing the chisel on the rest with the edge set at a shear angle of 45°, the heal of the bevel contacting the wood surface approx 1 in along from the end. It is possible to begin the cut at the end of the wood as with the deep fluted gouge, but it is much too difficult when learning with the skew. Much better to start a little way in where we have bevel support before the cutting edge enters the wood.

Place the steady hand on top of the tool so that it can press it firmly on the wood and the rest. Set the point of contact between the tool and the wood approx one third up the cutting edge from the bottom by varying the twist angle of the chisel as necessary. Around 10° of twist should be right. Don't worry about the position of the handle; if the cutting edge is in the right place then so is the handle. You don't think about the position of the steering wheel when driving a car, you just move it to keep the car on the road, and it's the

Figs 7.31 and 7.32 Tool rest set high for the large diameter but when the cut proceeds to the small diameter the tool needs to be raised into a difficult angle (7.33)

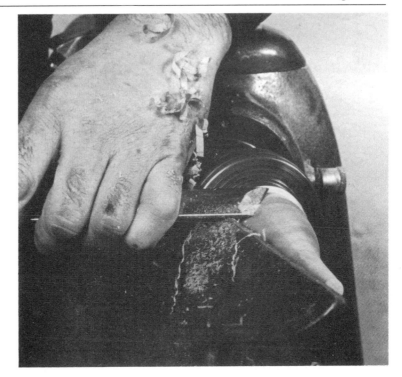

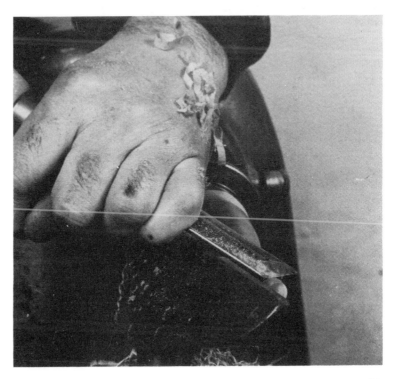

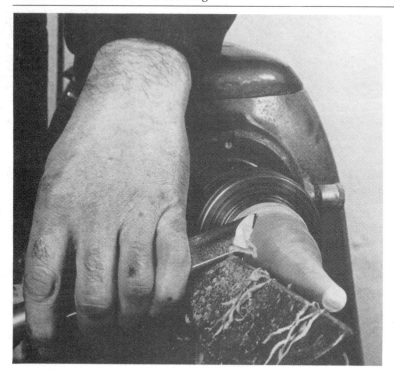

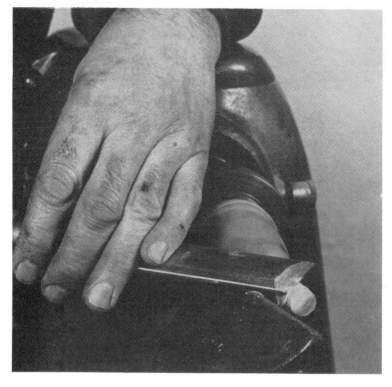

Figs 7.33 and 7.34 When the tool rest is set for the lowest diameter the tool is in a comfortable position for both diameters

Fig. 7.35

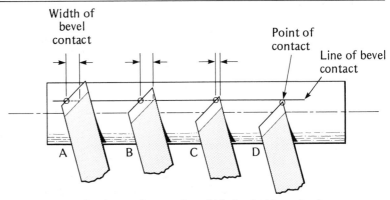

A. Cutting on lower edge of blade. Stable and safe.
B. Cutting higher on blade still stable and safe.
C. Cutting close to top. Bevel support reduced,
   too close to point for safety.
D. No bevel support. Will dig in immediately.

same here. I hope you are working from the tailstock end but it isn't essential. Stand behind the bevel looking in the direction of cut.

When cutting, the end of the tool is supported at two points, one corner of the tool on the rest, while the bevel lies on the workpiece behind the cutting edge, which will be in line with the top part of the edge which is cutting. Cutting will take place between these two points making it relatively stable. Using the lower half of the cutting edge only improves the stability and reduces the element of risk, which is how we want to start.

You will also notice that the bevel angle is very small, around 12–20°. This means that the major component of the pushing force along the handle will be in the direction of travel with only a small proportion at right angles to give stability against the wood. Additional support pressure is therefore required from the support hand to hold the tool against the wood and the rest.

Like the gouge, the bevel contact also provides a control surface about which the tool is pivoted for directional control.

Before switching on, make a few practice passes over the wood to get the feel of the movement and to get your feet and balance right. Swing the handle forward to make full bevel contact then slide the tool along the tool rest and wood, maintaining the same angle of presentation of tool to wood all the way. Go right to and off at the end.

When you are happy with the movement, start the lathe at around 1300 rpm and return to the ready position by setting up the angle of the cutting edge and making contact between the heel of the bevel. Swing the handle forward until full bevel contact is made then push the tool forward as in the practice run, the tool should again skim across the top of the surface without taking a cut. Repeat a few times to build confidence and the feel of control of the chisel.

To make a cut, what we want is the same movement again with the

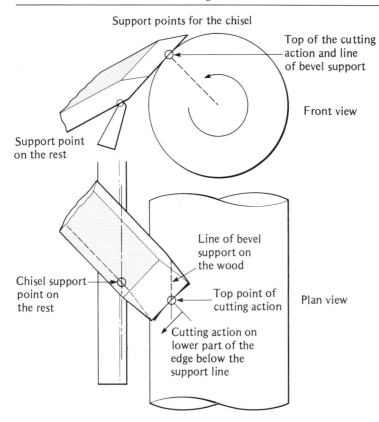

Support points for the chisel

Top of the cutting action and line of bevel support

Front view

Support point on the rest

Fig. 7.36 Varying 'shear' angle with a square edged chisel

Line of bevel support on the wood

Chisel support point on the rest

Top point of cutting action

Plan view

Cutting action on lower part of the edge below the support line

cutting edge just below the surface and removing a fine shaving. Switch on the lathe, place the tool in the start position then make full bevel contact, move the tool along as before and while doing so swing the handle forward about 10° of its start position, pivoting on the bevel. This will cause the edge to go into the wood. When it has gone in about $\frac{1}{32}$ in swing the handle back to its original angle while moving along, and continue to cut the wood to the end.

The width of the cutting edge in use should be about $\frac{3}{8}$ in and be about the initial contact point $\frac{1}{3}$ in from the bottom of the edge. If the cutting edge includes the lower point then all the cutting will be below the top surface of the wood and will require an increased feed pressure as well as producing a ragged edge in front of the tool. It isn't wrong to cut like that, just different and not what we want. If the cutting edge includes the top point, then all the bevel support is lost and the pressure on the tool will cause it to move uncontrollably into the wood, usually with a violent bang while ripping out a large chunk. To avoid this type of incident, leave out at least the top $\frac{1}{4}$ in, on this size of chisel, or any part of the edge which is above the point where the length of the bevel contact starts to reduce. While learning it is better to cut on the lower half of the cutting edge only.

Everything else being equal, the shavings should come off in long round twists and the finished surface be flat and smooth. Keep

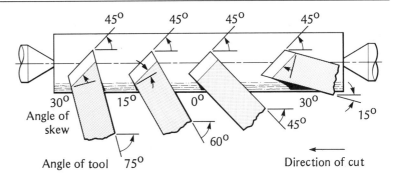

Fig. 7.37 Varying 'skew' angle for a fixed 'shear' angle, showing changes in tool position

repeating this cut till the wood is down to 1 in diameter, by which time you should have noticed that in order to maintain the cut on the same part of the edge, the tool handle had to be raised gradually to a higher position and twisted towards the wood. If you didn't do this then you will have found that the bottom point became embedded in the wood as the diameter reduced. Always watch the cutting edge and adjust it to maintain the point of cutting by moving the handle. The end which is still full size can be cut in the opposite direction. Repeat this exercise until you feel confident with the tool.

Put in another piece of wood, but this time make it tapered with the gouge, 2 in at the large end, 1 in at the other. To work with the grain, on the outside of a spindle, the cutting edge should face from the large diameter to the small.

With the lathe stopped, the tool rest at centre line height and parallel to the tapered surface, set the chisel on to the surface of the taper at the large end ready for a dummy run. Put a pencil line on the tool at the point where the edge makes contact on the wood, then run the tool along the wood as if making a cut, keeping the same shear angle and the same point of contact on the wood. Notice that the tool handle needs to be lifted and twisted to maintain these positions as the diameter reduces.

Get the feel of the tool movement and, when you can manage that without problems, try a cut, making the entry in the same way as before. Don't turn any of it to less than ¾ in diameter because we want to avoid vibrations and need to give additional support to the wood just now.

Repeat those exercises, making the cuts in the opposite direction, i.e. a change of hands. The procedure is just the same. Use as many pieces of wood as you think are necessary to gain complete confidence with the tool.

Now try precisely the same exercise with the skew chisel. Present the cutting edge at exactly the same shear angle to the wood. Which way up? Well it could be either way, but do it with the long point up first. You will notice that there are two differences from the square

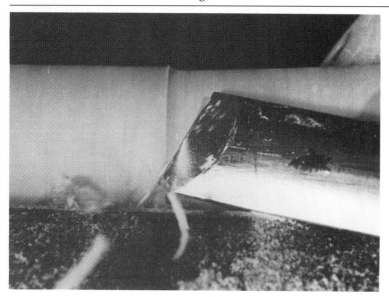

Fig. 7.38 Using the skew long point down

ground chisel, the length of the cutting edge is longer for the same width of tool, and in use the handle is at a different angle to the wood. Apart from that, everything else is exactly the same. Try all the above chisel exercises in that position until you feel happy with the tool.

For the third set of cuts turn the chisel round to the long point at the bottom, keeping the shear angle the same as before. Again you will notice that the handle is in a very different position from both the previous exercises, but the position of the cutting edge is identical. Repeat the set of exercises.

You should also have noted that as long as the cutting edge is presented correctly then it will cut irrespective of which way the handle is pointing. The position of the handle becomes important for the comfort and flexibility of handling for the turner. This is probably one of the main reasons why the skew is more popular than the square chisel, the other being its versatility with the two points at different angles.

Now that we have experienced both the skew and the square chisels we will continue with the skew only, long point up unless otherwise stated. Up to now we have been working with a shear angle of around 45°. This has only been a convenient starting angle which we can easily recognise. In practice the shear angle varies considerably with the wood and the situation. Try making a shear peeling cut as before, using the skew chisel long point up, starting with a shear angle of 45°, but this time swing the handle round to vary the shear angle as you go along. Maintain the same depth of cut on the lower half of the chisel and watch the points for digging-in.

Having made the most basic cuts with the chisel you should understand its method of use and feel fairly confident with the simple cuts. If I were to give you an axe, plane or other similar imple-

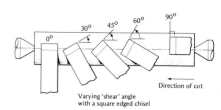

Varying 'shear' angle
with a square edged chisel

ment to use you would now understand how to present the cutting edge to the wood to make a successful long straight shear peeling cut. Not that you should try that, it is just a mental exercise.

It is very important to be confident and proficient with the chisel in making these long shear peeling cuts before proceeding to the next.

Determination, and possibly a bit of aggression, are also important ingredients. Let the wood and chisel know who is boss, be firm without being heavy handed (sounds almost like looking after young children) and with a little patience you can become much more relaxed and still get the response from the tool and wood. If you are in any doubt go back to the beginning of this chapter or even back to the deep fluted gouge.

Curves and chamfers

As we move round from cutting parallel to the axis to cutting square to the axis, the type of cutting changes from shear peeling to slicing. Now to accommodate this change the presentation of the cutting edge has to change.

It is at this stage I begin like a record, repeating myself because the cutting edge is doing exactly the same as the tip on the deep fluted gouge.

The differences as far as the turner is concerned are the handling characteristics of the skew which is much more unstable and a more difficult shape of stock to manipulate in the fingers.

For these shapes the skew can be used either way up.

Long point down
curves

Starting with the long point down, the tool rest $^3/_8$ in below the axis, skew horizontal and the stock vertical, curves can be made by just swinging the handle round. Now if we set up that situation with the bevel parallel to the axis, contacting a rounded piece with square ends between centres, and examine what we have, it will help us understand the cut and the tool movement.

Bringing the bevel into contact with the wood we see that the point of contact is at the same height as the axis and the shear angle the same as created by the angle of skew, (90° − skew angle = shear angle).

Now if we swing the tool round 90°, lining up the bevel on the square end, we see that the cutting action has changed from shear peeling to slicing without altering the angle of the cutting edge. We can't see just now because the whole cuting edge is in contact with the wood, but when it is rounded, the point of cutting will be lower on the cutting edge, i.e. below the axis. Now this tells us that we can make the curve by just swinging the handle.

In practice, I have found that towards the end of the curve when the cutting is below the axis, there is a tendency for the lower half of the tool to be twisted into the wood, causing a dig-in. Now this can be avoided if the tool is inclined slightly onto the wood from the start, then the handle is raised to make the cutting edge vertical towards the end of the cut to maintain the point of cutting at axis height. This method works well on large curves but can be clumsy on small ones. When making this cut on an unsupported end, the pip in the centre can be sliced off very neatly. The curved skew is also very good for this cut.

Long point down
chamfers

A chamfer is a flat profile at an angle to the axis, with a sharp change in direction at either end. The cutting and exit are very much the same as the curve. The difference is in the entry which itself changes as the chamfer angle is increased. Staying with the chisel long point down and the rest below the axis as above we can now make chamfers.

First try a chamfer of between 10 and 20°, not that the exact angle really matters as long as it is small, (less than 45°). It's more a matter of planning the cuts, executing them and achieving the results for which confidence and firm control are needed.

Set the tool horizontally on the rest at the end of the wood, point the bevel at the angle of chamfer, set to take a small cut, when ready, start the lathe and push the tool forward into the wood. Once bevel

Fig. 7.39 Making entry with the long point to establish bevel support

Fig. 7.40 Bevel support established, cutting edge lowered to slicing cut

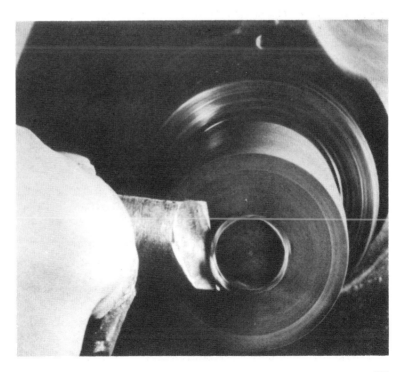

Fig. 7.41 Continuing slicing cut

Fig. 7.42 Slice removed almost whole

contact is made, the steady hand should hold the tool firmly onto the wood and follow the cut through. Subsequent cuts are just a repeat of this procedure. Very simple with no problems.

Now, that is fine for small angles where the cutting is shear peeling; for angles around 45° and above, there are two changes.

The same entry can still be used, with care, but there is sometimes a tendency for the tool to skid across the surface creating groves. This can be avoided by lowering the handle until the initial point of contact is the long point, then entry is made by pushing the point into the wood. Once entry is complete and bevel contact established then the handle should be raised to the horizontal position and the slicing cut continued.

As the cut nears the axis the finishing can be a little easier if the handle is raised to bring the point of cutting nearer to axis level.

This is OK for chamfers up to about 85°, above that the clearance between the cutting edge and the finished face is too small for comfort and at 90° the whole of the cutting edge is in contact with the wood, which is very dangerous. The curved skew gives more clearance and can be used right up to 90°.

Long point up chamfers

Raise the tool rest to axis height or thereabouts. With the long point up, set the bevel in the direction of the chamfer, between 10 and 20° and the shear angle at around 70°. Bring the tool up to the wood and check that the point of contact between the wood and the cutting edge is between a quarter and a third of this way up the edge from the bottom of the tool when it is leaned over slightly onto the wood. Hold the stock in the support hand with an overhand grip, the heal of the hand firmly pressed against the rest. (This hand grip is used for firmness when the tool movement is more along the wood than towards the axis). You are now ready to try a cut, just a small one about $\frac{1}{32}$ in from the end. The initial insertion is the most critical part of the cut because if it is made wrong then, at best, the corner won't be sharp and at worst, which is most likely, the chisel will be kicked back along the surface causing deep scoring to the finished surface.

The entry should be very firm and positive, using the tool rest and the body to support the chisel. Once it is in, the bevel will be in the support and the tool held firmly against the wood with the steady hand. It is just a matter of following through to the end of the first short cut.

The second and subsequent cuts are made in a similar fashion. As the diameter at the end of the chamfer is reducing it will be necessary to raise and twist the tool to maintain the correct cutting position and shear angle on the chisel. Stop when the diameter is reduced to 1 in.

Again for chamfer angles around 45° and above it is advisable not only to change the method of entry but also the method of grip. An underhand grip with the index finger anchored around the tool rest and the tool held between the other fingers and thumb.

Set the chisel on the rest with the bevel pointing in the direction of the chamfer in a position where the point of contact is one third up from the lower corner. Lower the handle until the initial contact is made with the lower point, the short point, push the tool forward to make the entry then raise the handle again to the initial position with the slicing cut on the lower part of the edge. Now as the cut proceeds, continue to raise the handle to maintain the cut on the same part of the edge.

This cut can be used up to a chamfer angle of 85°, with a straight edged skew. The round edged skew can be used right up to the 90° chamfer, (square shoulder).

**Long point up
curves**

Shallow curves can be introduced while making straight peeling cuts by twisting the chisel very slightly. This alters the direction the bevel is pointing and therefore the direction of cut. Again it will be noticed that as the bevel is twisted towards the axis, the point of cutting moves down the edge. This can be counteracted by lifting the handle to maintain the cutting position. Twisting in the opposite direction will produce a concave curve.

Alternatively the same shallow curves can be achieved by simply swinging the handle forwards, again changing the direction of the bevel and therefore the direction of cut. Try both of these methods, keep the depth of cut shallow and the shear angle around 60° at the start.

Making a full quadrant is quite a different problem, with a lot of swinging and twisting of the tool. If we take the start position as for making a shear peeling cut with a shear angle around 60° and the finish position with the bevel at 90° to the axis and the cutting edge tangential to the axis, then we can see the swing and twist required of the tool and that we are back to requiring fine delicate control.

The smaller the radius of the curve the more delicate the movement and control. For the first one round off the end of a 2 in diameter piece of wood making a radius of about 1 in.

Set the tool in the start position with a shear angle around 45–60° contacting the wood about one third of the way up the cutting edge, holding it in the underhand grip with the index finger anchored round the tool rest and the tool stock held in the fingertips. The drive hand is the control hand, the steady hand acts like a brake to improve the control.

The first cut will be a very short one, not requiring much twist or swing, but this will increase as the curve gets bigger. The point of cutting will move down the edge as the cut gets deeper, unless compensated for by raising the handle. We don't want the bottom corner cutting as this will reduce the quality of the finish. Practise the cut very slowly, almost in slow motion, not only to show that you have complete control over the situation but so that you can watch the cut proceed and understand what is happening. This requires more force from both hands which are fighting against each other. Progress to smaller curves as you feel more confident.

Pointing

Pointing is a very different method of cutting the wood. It is just the points that pierces the wood while the very edge of the bevel on the finish side provides the control surface and the edge of the bevel on the waste side pushes off the waste as the widening tool tries to fit into the pierced line of the point. It is done with both long and short point of the skew chisel and is used for cutting 'V's, squaring ends, shoulders, chamfers, rounding corners and beading, i.e. most forms of detail cut.

As the cutting action is on the tip only, then the rest of the cutting edge must be kept away from the cut face. It must also be kept away from the waste on the other side. If it catches either of these then a dig-in will result, causing the tool to cut a deep gouge from the wood.

To understand the cutting process a little more before trying it with the skew, it is better to start with a special tool. It is not available in the shops but is simple to make. Take a $\frac{1}{4}$ diameter round bar, 8–10 in long and sharpen the end just like a pencil, this will represent the point of the skew without the long cutting edge. You could go a little better and grind an old worn out round stock HSS chisel for a better point. I made my first one from a 4 in nail, although a masonry nail would have been superior. Whichever you choose, it is a very simple and effective tool. Don't forget a handle.

You know which way the tool is pointing because it is round, and all ways up are the same, like the skew it has two bevels, one either side.

It's magic tool for squaring ends and making chamfers and 'V's, all straight line cutting.

To show the true qualities of the tool, practise on a straight, close-grained hard wood such as sycamore, beech, or the soft wood yew. Try a chamfer to start with, about 60–70°. With the tool rest at axis height and a round piece of wood between centres, place the tool on the rest, line up the bevel on the wood side of the tool with the angle of the chamfer and stand looking down the bevel just like any other tool. Hold the tool underhand between fingers and thumb with the index finger anchored round the tool rest, this hold should now becoming automatic for detail work.

As this tool only pierces a line, the amount of wood that can be removed at one time is limited to around $\frac{1}{16}$ in but it is better to start with less than half of that. The point could be pushed in horizontally and it will cut. Raising the point slightly, 10–20°, will greatly improve the cutting action. To make the cut, simply push the point into the wood, once entry is made then the steady hand holds the tool firmly against the cut face. Lower the point as the cut approaches the axis. Taking the cut slowly will produce acceptable results on soft woods and very fine results on hard woods. Repeat the cut until the chamfer is complete. Amazingly simple, with no risk of dig-ins whatsoever.

Having successfully made a chamfer, that is all there is to using the tool. Squaring ends, even working along the surface is possible. To make a 'V', the first cut is square into the centre to create space for subsequent cuts, which are made exactly as the chamfer on alternate sides.

This tool has possibilities in its own right. Very fine detail is possible, particularly on small work, possibly miniature. It also gives access to cuts which are not possible with any other cutting tool.

With all this going for the tool it ought to be christened. As my first one was made from a nail I will call it 'The nail'.

Returning to skew

'Pointing' with the skew is almost identical to pointing with the nail, but with the problem of the long cutting edge which must be kept away from the wood at all costs. At the moment, my results from the skew are better than with the nail particularly on soft woods. Could improving the material of my nail make up the difference, or is the very end of the cutting edge on the skew playing some part?

Trying to relate the skew to the nail has just one problem. Which way is the skew pointing? There are two choices, the first is to take the half of the angle at the point which looks fairly obvious, or take it as the direction of the lower edge which is on the rest. The second option appears to meet all the practical requirements of the process

Fig. 7.43 Path of the cutting point as it squares the end

and is easier to describe. Not that it makes a great deal of difference anyway.

Need I say more on making chamfers? Use the long point of the skew. If you can do it with the nail then you can do it with the skew; it is precisely the same procedure. Squaring ends and shoulders are also done in exactly the same way. Don't forget to stand looking down the bevel and keep the cutting edge away from the wood.

The short point can also make the same cuts in exactly the same way, but the end of the tool needs to be raised much higher for the point to make contact and the view of the cutting is reduced because the long point is up.

Fig. 7.44 Making entry with the long point squaring the end

Fig. 7.45 Continuing pointing cut, following a trajectory to the centre point

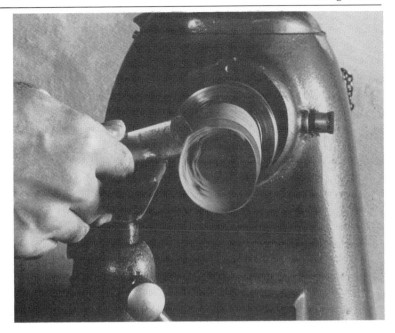

Curves

Pointing with the skew is more versatile than with the nail. It can cut curves in the form of beads or round corners, if we use the short point, because it is only this point which gives us the bevel control behind the cutting edge in this rolling cut. The cutting action is just the same but the flat face of the bevel is used to control the movement, not the bottom edge.

The real secret in making the rolling cut with the short point is stability, flexibility and control. Functions which are just the same as for any detail cut. Use a softwood to practise on, as this will reduce the cutting forces and make practice easier. The first step is to plan the cuts, take a 2 in diameter × 6 in long piece of straight grained wood between centres to make a $\frac{1}{2}$ in radius curve on the corners at either end. If you are right-handed, start at the right-hand end, left-handed at the left-hand end. Set the tool rest roughly level with the bottom of the curve ($\frac{1}{2}$ in above axis) with the support post well away from the corner so that the first finger can be hooked underneath the rest, providing a firm anchor point to give stability. You might have been able to guess that that is the way to hold the tool.

Up to now we have been using 1 in or $1\frac{1}{4}$ in skew chisels which are ideal for the shear peeling cuts on 2 in wood. The pointing cut used for detail work can be accomplished safely using smaller chisels, because the action is at one end of the cutting edge only and there is less likelihood of the other point coming into contact with the wood. You can continue with the large chisel, although the rolling movement may be easier with a smaller one, say a $\frac{3}{4}$ in. The chisel movement is a rolling action from the top to the bottom of the corner,

Fig. 7.46 Skew chisel set to take the second cut rounding the end. The first finger is hooked under the tool rest for stability and firm control. The tool is held between the end of the thumb and the fingertips for ease of manipulation

which requires fine control, combined with a slide across the rest.

As it is the short point that is going to be doing the cutting, that should take the lead in the direction of cut. It should also be the point of contact between the tool and the wood. The cut starts with the chisel just a few degrees off the square to the axis pointing in the direction of travel, in what is almost a peeling cut position with very little shear, but with the blade pushed further over the wood so that only the short point of the edge is catching the surface. In this position the bevel is rubbing along the surface from the short point back-

Fig. 7.47 Cut started by twisting the tool and moving forward at the same time

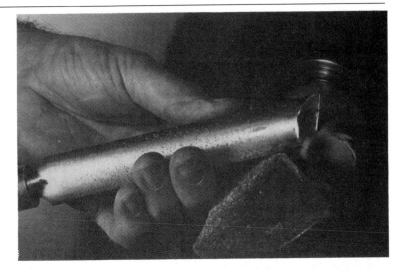

Fig. 7.48 Tool almost vertical towards the end of cut. The tool twist has been made with the control hand while the stability hand held the bevel hard onto the wood and acted as a break on the tip movement

Fig. 7.49 Pointing cut with the chisel

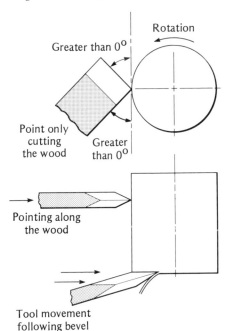

Pointing at the end of the wood. Note the clearance angle created between the long cutting edge and the wood by the angle of the tool.

wards, axially along the wood, and there is an angle of clearance between the wood and the cutting edge which is naturally created by the angle of skew.

Before making the cut, move the point to the end of the wood and twist the tool into the finish position with the control hand to see the total tool movement required. The steady hand provides some resistance to the movement, which improves the control. Practise the movement until it feels comfortable.

The cut is a pointing cut which starts and finishes as such, so, in the final position, it is the short point only of the tool which is to contact the bottom of the bead. This means that angle between the cutting edge and the radius to the point must be greater than 90°, say 100° or the cutting edge will contact the bottom first in a slicing cut. The bevel on the wood side should be square to the axis when finishing off the corner.

Make the first cut $\frac{1}{8}$ in from the end and following cuts at $\frac{1}{4}$, $\frac{3}{8}$ in and the final cut at $\frac{1}{2}$ in. For more practice, repeat the final cut every $\frac{1}{16}$ in all the way along the wood, concentrating on the rolling action and the shape of the corner. Don't worry about the mess that is being left behind.

Repetition like this is the ideal practice and gives you plenty of time to sort out any problems. Repeat the exercise on another piece of wood, working from the other end. This will be slightly different as you will have to work towards yourself or change hands. Being able to work in both directions with the same hands will make beading quicker.

'V's, beads and square shoulders

The exercises we have done with the skew enable us to make all the necessary cuts, but there is a little more to know about specific applications to particular shapes, such as 'V's, beads and square shoulders.

Cutting 'V's

Making a 'V' is exactly the same as making two facing chamfers which meet up at the bottom, using either a pointing or slicing cut. The first problem will be space, because we are working in the middle of a piece of wood that will not yield. Clearing space for the chisel to work is done gradually, first by making the initial tool insertion at the centre of the 'V'. For example, if we are making the 'V' with the pointing cut with the long point then we would proceed as follows: the tool could be set horizontally on the rest and pushed in a direct line towards the centre, the clearance angle required to fit in the tool would be the angle of the tool. Alternatively the tip could be raised to a point where it is tangential to the surface and the entry made there. From this position as the point enters the wood, the full thickness of the chisel would quickly follow the tip, requiring almost an 180° clearance angle to fit the tool in.

Penetration would be minimal, if at all. Between these two extreme positions the clearance angle required by the tool at the point of entry will vary according to the angle at which the tool is presented to the wood.

For the initial cut we want maximum penetration to make as much clearance as possible for the following cuts and from the above we see that this will be achieved by pushing the tool in horizontally. Because the tool can only score a line to create clearance and cannot remove any waste, don't push it in too far or for too long. The tip is liable to overheat and destroy the point.

Subsequent entries can be made with the point raised as for chamfers. The point should follow a trajectory to bring it horizontal at the end of each cut for maximum penetration and maximum clearance of the waste.

Cuts are made on alternate sides and, as for previous 'V's, stand slightly to one side of the 'V' to allow room for the tool to swing from one side to the other, and make all the cuts either left or right-handed. Be sure you are in a position to see the cut. The grip should be underhand, leaning firmly on the rest or the anchor grip, so that the tool can be manipulated in the fingers without obscuring the view of the cutting.

Take a 2 in diameter round piece about 12 in long between centres to make a series of 'Vs' along its length. Set the tool rest at centre line height. It could be higher but I prefer this height because it eliminates the necessity of raising the tool handle up above the horizontal when coming to the bottom of a 'V' or close to the centre when squaring the end.

The narrowest 'V' we can make is the angle of the chisel, (about 25°) but it is advisable to make it slightly wider to allow space to clear the waste. For practice, let's make it about 35° (or 10° wider than the chisel). Don't make them too deep or the wood will be weakened

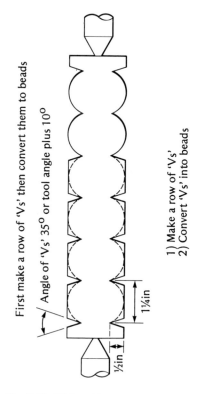

Fig. 7.50 'V's and beads

106

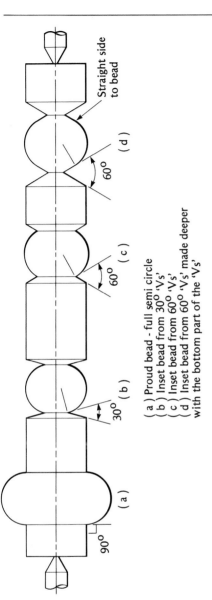

Straight side to bead

(d)

60°

(c)

60°

30°

(b)

(a) Proud bead - full semi circle
(b) Inset bead from 30° 'V's'
(c) Inset bead from 60° 'V's'
(d) Inset bead from 60° 'V's' made deeper
    with the bottom part of the 'V'

(a)

90°

Fig.7.51 Beads

beyond use, say $\frac{1}{2}$ in deep on 2 in round which will give a width of approx $\frac{1}{2}$ in. Now we have the size of the 'V's. If we mark them out 1 in between centres, they can be converted into bead in the next exercise.

If it does not come out right first time, don't try to doctor it, go on to the next one and the next one . . .

Square shoulders

The square face can be made with the pointing cut, or using the curved skew with the slicing cut. Most of the cut parallel to the axis can be made with the shear peeling, but as the tool approaches the shoulder the lower point will catch the face. If we turn the tool to 90° shear the edge will get into the corner but the whole of the edge will contact the face and dig in. There are two ways around this problem, the first is to push the tool up on the wood, as the cut approaches the corner, until the cut is a pointing cut with the lower point which will then clean the corner.

The second is to use a curved skew turned to 90° shear in the centre of the tool which will take a fine cut right into the corner.

Beads

For recessed beads, 'V's are cut first then converted using the cut for round corners. All the cuts are made on one side first and then the other. Try converting the 'V's made earlier into beads. Proud beads are made by converting specially prepared shoulders. The most difficult cut to make on a bead is the last one because there can be a tendency to flatten the top. This is avoided by very careful initial contact and control.

Scrapers

Scraping is a cutting action where the cutting edge is at 90° to the surface being cut and has a burr on the end which is created in the grinding. This is a statement which is generally accepted in wood turning without being questioned, tested or examined. While it would take microscopic examination to determine the true nature of the cutting action, there is no doubt that it is effective for many situations and while we might not fully understand the precise nature of the cutting, there are many practical aspects to be considered for efficient use of the tool.

Surprising though it may seem, I have more scrapers than gouges. While the amount of use they get is very little, they are an essential tool to have in my collection. The reason why I have so many is that they are a specific tool, i.e. shaped for a particular job or situation without very much versatility, even between sizes of a particular shape. They tend to be used for shaping, smoothing or removing waste where other tools cannot operate.

They are and look a very crude and simple tool but require a lot of thought and respect when using them. They can put the final touches to a masterpiece or destroy it in the blink of an eye. One can almost tell by looking at the tool how to use it, not realising the hidden dangers ready to take advantage of the unwary.

As with other tools the scraper can be used for removing considerable amounts of waste but it is the smoothing and finishing cuts we are mainly concerned with. From the exercises we have already done with gouges, most of the wood has been removed by scraping, so why is it that a tool that only removes wood by scraping is so very different? Just to remind us, a few notes on the scraping cuts of the gouge for comparison:

a) the scraping edge is being pushed very positively forward into the wood to be removed.

d) the scraping action is on the waste face not the finish face, therefore the finish which is very often rough, does not matter and any scraping dig-in would not damage the finish wood.

e) the length of cutting edge scraping is very short i.e with a $\frac{1}{2}$ in deep cut the scraping edge in action will only be about $\frac{3}{8}$ in which keeps the downward pressure on the tip to a minimum and is easily counteracted by the leverage of the long handle.

b) the tool is held very firmly in place by the presure down the long handle from the control hand holding the bevel against the finished face of the wood and the support hand pulling the tool onto the rest.

e) with gouges there are usually quite a number of cuts to be made which act as a form of warm-up to the final cut. When using the scraper for smoothing there may only be one critical cut to make, which has to be done from 'cold', getting it right first time.

The tool in use

The purpose of the scraper is:

a) to smooth surfaces left by previous tools, i.e. ripples inside a bowl left by a gouge, using a shape of scraper similar to the surface being cut.

b) to refine shapes and blend in curves from other tools.

c) to remove waste where access is not possible with gouges.

d) to work areas where dimensional tolerances or form are critical. i.e. joint faces for lids of boxes, or in the work of a pattern maker or musical instrument maker.

The scraping action requires a large downwards force by the rotating wood onto the tool to effect a cut. This force is proportional to the

Fig. 7.52 Choosing the right scraper

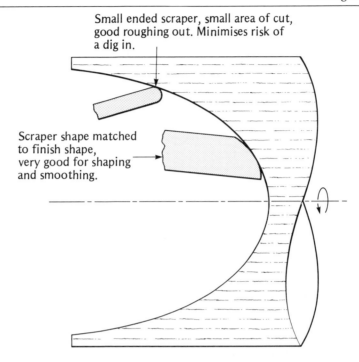

Small ended scraper, small area of cut, good roughing out. Minimises risk of a dig in.

Scraper shape matched to finish shape, very good for shaping and smoothing.

length of cutting edge in contact with the wood. The depth of cut also affects the force but this is limited by the ability of the tool. A short cutting edge generates the smallest forces and is therefore the easiest to operate. This is ideal for the roughing out process, especially where very long overhangs are involved such as in tall hollow vessels where quality of finish is secondary.

To produce a long smooth surface with a fine finish then a long smooth cutting edge of a similar shape is required. The nearer the shape of the tool to the finish shape the easier it is to turn the shape. This would result in a very long cutting edge in contact with the wood and generate large forces even for fine cuts. A practical solution is to use a shape of tool which is similar in shape to the curve required and limit the length of contact to about $\frac{1}{2}$ in or less, even this taking a cut $\frac{1}{32}$ in deep will generate greater forces than the gouge taking a $\frac{1}{2}$ in deep cut, which is a hefty one indeed. Depth control needs to be very precise as a small increase in thickness of cut would increase the width of the cut considerably and this could be impossible to control with a standard handle. There is a depth of cut beyond which the scraping action breaks down, which could result (depending upon the conditions at the time) in:

1. With limited power at the lathe and using a good long handle, the rotation of the wood will be stopped.
2. With more power, the lathe will continue to rotate but the tool will tear the grain very badly.

109

3. With adequate power and a short handle the tool may be drawn further into the wood as it is tipped out of the control of the operator, from which anything could happen.

The results of taking too wide a cut would be similar.

To produce a refined shape with a good finish the scraper is drawn or pushed gently over the surface, taking very fine shavings. The tool movement for cutting feed and shape is controlled by both hands drawing (or pushing) the cutting edge along the surface of the wood with some feedback from the cutting edge. As there is no bevel rubbing about which to pivot, any change in direction of the cutting edge is from a combination of feel and of manoeuvering the tool with both hands.

I find the tool control much easier when the handle is offset from the surface, i.e. skewed at an angle as when using a gouge or chisel so that the handle is in front of or behind the cutting edge depending on whether it is being pushed or pulled. With the cutting edge skewed it also gives a longer edge over which the curvature can vary to suit more situations.

Stability for the scraper is achieved by placing the tool flat on the rest and holding it down very firmly with the support hand with a long handle to the control hand. Because we don't have any stability from the contact between the tool and the wood, more pressure between tool and tool rest, together with a longer handle than is the case with the gouge, are needed. A heavy scraper makes a considerable contribution to the stability.

The contact between the tool and the wood should be like two large heavy bodies brushing past each other with a small overlap, whereas with the gouge, the two large bodies are leaning heavily on each other as they pass with an overlap.

Setting the tool rest is probably that most important part in the preparation for using the scraper. The idea is to set the height and position so that any sudden force on the tip, moving it downwards, will not result in the tool being drawn further into the wood.

First, the closer the better, giving negligible leverage at the tip end, which is easily counteracted by minimal force at the end of a long handle. This is usually easy enough on the outside of a form, but as in goblets, egg cups, deep narrow boxes, bowls where there is not room inside for both tool and rest then a considerable overhang will result. Again, the long handle is essential. In any situation, to guarantee that the tip will move away from the wood when pivoted downwards on the rest, the cutting angle must be 90° or more and the distance from tool tip to the support point on the rest must be less than the radius of the curve being cut. The sketches show various situations which work and others that do not, also the effect of the thickness of the tool which is considerable in a tight situation. The grain is also a significant factor in the risk of problems, on side grain such as the straight sides of a goblet the grain is uniform, presenting little risk. On the end grain such as at the bottom of the goblet the risk is increased.

The greatest risk is on the inside of bowls where the grain con-

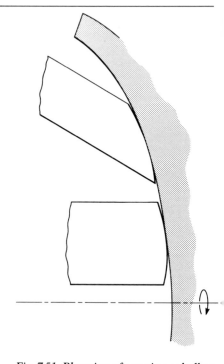

Fig. 7.51 Plan view of scraping a shallow bowl

Fig. 7.52 Scraper tip movement and risk of 'dig-in'

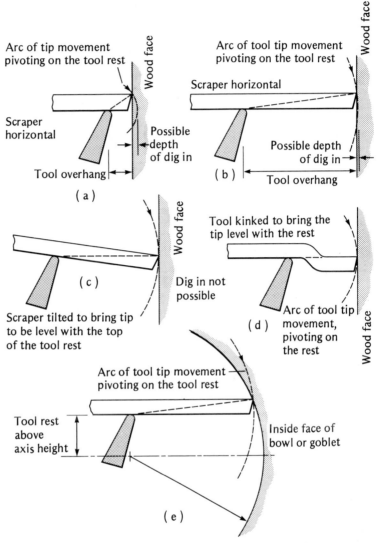

(a) Very small overhang therefore risk of dig in small
but if it does happen it can be very deep.
(b) Large overhang therefore high risk of dig in
but if it happens the dig in will be small.
(c,d) Dig in not possible because tip lowered to rest level
(e) Risk reduced inside bowl by raising tool rest above axis height.

stantly changes from end to side and much of the cutting is against the grain. Placing the rest close to the wood in many bowl shapes is difficult, again making a long handle essential.

Applications

For the pattern maker, accuracy of size and shape are essential. A

111

good finish, though desirable, is secondary and can be more a function of how the blank is built up rather than the tool used to turn. For this kind of work the scraper is the tool to produce the results because it can skim very light shavings either all over or in a local spot to refine shape and size to a considerable degree of accuracy.

On outside spindle work where the look to the eye and the feel of the hand are the judges, there is no place for scrapers because all the necessary shapes and cuts can be made much more efficiently, effectively and leaving a far superior finish with either gouges or chisels. The temptation just to skim a form with the scraper if the previous cuts have not gone according to plan should be resisted as you will come to rely on it rather than learn to use the chisels and gouges correctly. There are a few exceptions: boxes and spigots where a precise size is needed for the perfect fit.

Egg cups, goblets, boxes are tight hollow forms turned along the grain, where the use of gouges is restricted in operating space. Also, to work with the grain they would have to cut from the base to the rim, a cut with which form control is lost because the bevel cannot rub behind the cutting edge. A job for the scraper to finish off.

Scrapers can be used to smooth out any ripples on bowls and platters caused by difficult grain or to blend in the centre pip which is sometimes difficult with a gouge. Another situation where they are indispensable is making recesses on the base of bowls and platters for a chuck to fit. The list of situations where scrapers are valuable is quite endless, with each case requiring a specific tool.

Don't be tempted to use the chisels on their sides as scrapers because the cutting edge required is different and the fine edge used for peeling will very quickly be destroyed and it will take some time to restore it. Also, the corners at the heel of the bevel created by the sharpening on both sides, get in the way when working internally.

First cuts

Start with a piece of 2 in × 2 in × 6 in which has been roughed down, and mounted in a chuck at one end. While we should hollow out the centre with a small gouge, for practice we will use a scraper. Do not use a drill for this job, it is slow, expensive on drills, and leaves a shape we don't want.

First, find a $\frac{3}{8}$ in round ended scraper (about $\frac{5}{16}$ in thick) which is at least 4 in long, but preferably longer, with a long handle. Set the tool rest $\frac{1}{2}$ in away from the end and so the top of the tool will be $\frac{1}{8}$ in above the centre height.

Sharpen the tool and approach the lathe. It should be obvious where to stand. Right hip against the bed looking on to the end to be hollowed out, tool in right hand with the left hand holding it on the rest. If your lathe bed is 30 in or less in length it is a good idea to remove the tailstock as this will get in the way of the elbow. The few minutes it takes will be more than made up for with the easier access. The initial contact between tool and wood must be very slow and gentle. Sudden contact can cause snatching and torn grain. Set the

Fig. 7.53 Scraping the inside of a goblet or egg cup

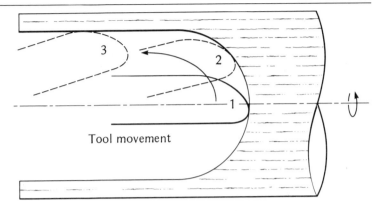

Tool movement

Grain running along the length,
working from short to long grain

Fig. 7.54 Making a flat face with the scraper

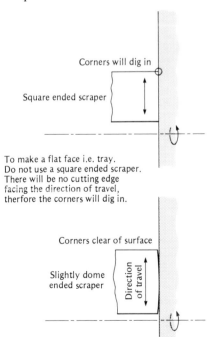

Corners will dig in

Square ended scraper

To make a flat face i.e. tray.
Do not use a square ended scraper.
There will be no cutting edge
facing the direction of travel,
therfore the corners will dig in.

Corners clear of surface

Slightly dome
ended scraper

Direction
of travel

tool firmly on the rest and raise the handle to bring the centre down to centre height and push it $\frac{1}{8}$ in into the centre of the wood. Draw it out as if it were following the final shape, swinging the handle round slightly to keep the cutting on the tip and minimise the length of edge cutting. Repeat this procedure for subsequent cuts and at a depth of $\frac{1}{2}$ in move the rest as close as possible to the workpiece. Continue hollowing out to a depth of $1\frac{1}{2}$ in and a diameter of $1\frac{1}{2}$ in at the mouth. Chose a rounded end scraper roughly the finish shape we want and a size which will fit easily into the hollow. Check that the metal below the cutting edge is ground away enough so as not to interfere with the wood. Set the tool rest across the mouth of the hollow at a height so that the top of the tool will be about $\frac{1}{8}$ in above centre. The cut has to be made from the centre in the base to the rim to be with the grain. Put the tool on the rest, push it in to the centre, raising the handle to bring the tip in line with the centre. When contact is made, swing the tool lightly backwards and forwards over the centre, pivoting in the hand at the rest, and take a few shavings off the centre $\frac{1}{2}$ in. This is done with the tip of the tool. Continue the cut to the rim by drawing the tool across the bottom and up the side. At the same time gradually change the position of the cut on the tool from the tip for cutting at the bottom to the side of the tool for the straight section to the rim. The handle should also be gradually lowered to the horizontal, as the cutting edge moves away from the centre. Repeat this cut until the wall thickness is down to $\frac{1}{8}$ in. As it gets thinner, chatter may become a problem, which we want to avoid just now. Part off the hollow section and start again, and again, and again.

In the situation where a square lip or very staight sides are needed, then a different scraper is used; one with a square end, and sharpened on the side as well as the end. This time the tool is pushed in from the rim parallel to the lathe axis.

To make an area flat, a wide very slightly domed scraper is used. It would not be possible to draw a flat ended scraper across the surface

113

Fig. 7.55 Parting tool.

because of the corners and if it were jabbed in to give a series of flat surfaces then these would need blending in.

Smoothing off the inside of a bowl with a scraper should only be necessary when the shape does not allow complete gouge control or the wood is particularly difficult. The procedure would be very much the same as the first scraper. Practise using the smoothing scraper. I find control of the scraper much easier when working from base to rim.

My favourite scrapers are flat bars of silver steel between 1 in and 2 in wide, $\frac{3}{16}$ in thick and 6 in long and sharpened in various shapes at one end. They are for use hand held *without* a rest. They can be used in two ways. First, with the tool square to the face but with a steep cutting angle and supported by a finger underneath. A very fine cut can be taken, without any risk of digging-in, leaving a good finish. This is ideal for blending in curves and refining shapes. The second is to hold it to cut in shear; the angle can be varied greatly depending on the situation. I find this useful on the insides of bowls for very fine cuts on very thin work. The tool should be held so with the handle end outside the bowl, so that it cannot catch the wood, which would be very dangerous. Conventional gouges can be used in the same manner but are just slightly clumsier. A good selection of scrapers is needed for versatility. Always keep a few blanks in hand ready to be shaped for a particular job.

Parting tools

Parting tools do exactly as the name says. They part two pieces of wood. Which particular parting tool is used depends upon the application. The standard parting tool looks very much like a thin slice from a chisel, this is suitable for most situations and particularly when using expensive woods. A very thin tool will only waste a small amount of wood.

SAFETY

The wood turner's workshop is a very dangerous place to be; power saws, sharp chisels and rotating pieces of wood etc present very obvious dangers and the results are instantaneous. Safety precautions are usually fairly obvious and many of them pure common sense. There is also a degree of built-in safety in the design of machines, with recommended methods of installation and use advised by the manufacturers. Always follow these as standard workshop procedure in order to minimise risks.

There are however, the more insidious dangers of noise and fine dust in the workshop, dangers which are not immediately obvious. There is no pain to show that damage is being done, damage for which there is no cure. The results of intermitent or continuous exposure do not become apparent for many years, by which time it is too late to be thinking in terms of precautions.

Noise

Noise is a nuisance, and often that is all it is. But as noise levels increase they gradually change to being injurious to our hearing. We are not able to recognise this change because there is no pain associated with the damage. Duration of exposure is also a factor when calculating the total damage, low noise levels over a long period can be just as damaging as high noise over a much shorter period.

The long term effects of exposure to noise can be premature loss of hearing, a prospect none of us would look forward to.

It won't happen to me (so we all think), but most of the equipment in a woodturners workshop emits noise which will cause damage over a period, so we should all be taking precautions of some kind irrespective of how small our operation.

Precautions can be very easy, cheap and effective:

1. Distance. Keep as far away as is practicable from the source. This costs nothing if you have the space, but is often impossible because the noise is generated by the machine you are using. Other pieces of equipment like compressors and dust extractors can be remotely situated more easily.

116

2. Protection. Wear ear muffs, these are very cheap and very effec- tive, They do have disadvantages. Listening to the radio or talking to the man on the next machine are more difficult but that is a small price to pay.

   Try a little test, put on a pair of muffs before switching on and carrying out your noisiest operation. In the middle of it, take off the muffs and feel the shock of the noise. You will be quite amazed at the difference and will think twice about doing the operation without them in the future. Some are better than others so try them on at the door of the shop to test the difference.

3. Noise suppression. This can be possible on certain types of equipment by shielding with some form of sound insulator, but take expert advice to be sure that machines don't overheat and create a fire hazard!

Dust

The other silent intruder is dust, produced in profusion from all kinds of woodturning machinery, in particular turning and sanding. Unlike noise, it does not disappear when you switch off the machine. The dust floats around in the atmosphere for hours and then settles only to be disturbed again later. On a bright sunny day look at the dust in the sun's rays coming through the window, remembering that the dust is all through the workshop and not just in the rays where it can be seen, and it does not go in with the sun, it is there all the time.

To many people the dust isn't even a nuisance except when they can't find something because it is completely covered in dust.

In the short term part of the air passages can become sensitised to other forms of dust, particularly house dust, then there is no escaping from the problem. The dust can cause respiratory prob- lems similar to asthma. Some woods are carcinogenic and can cause cancer of the nasal and sinus passages. A long-term heritage for the future. But it is not just the dust from wood that can be a problem; particles from the garnet paper and the glue which hold it to the backing, the finishes we apply and sand down afterwards, fungus and spores from decaying wood, all these are floating around in the atmosphere and pass easily into and out of our lungs as we breathe. We take in approx 1 cu ft of air per minute at work, that's 60 cu ft/hr, or 480 cu ft/working day. That can be an awful lot of dust.

Steps to reduce the hazard should be related to the size of the problem. Wearing a mask is the front line defence and is a must where any dust is created. In general the better the mask the more bulky it is and restrictive on visibility. While I would recommend you to wear the most effective mask you can buy, it is better to buy a mask that you will wear all the time and feel comfortable. I wear the martindale foil mask with renewable filters which I change 3 or 4 times a day.

The other front line defence would be one of the clean air hoods which blows filtered air over the face, I haven't tried one, but if it is

117

the only form of dust control then it should be worn all the time in the dusty workshop.

My latest piece of safety equipment is a 2 gallon watering can, ideal for keeping down the dust when cleaning up after a day's work. It makes an enormous difference to the atmosphere.

The next line of defence is some form of extraction. A fan in the window will be a good help but slow in clearing the air. The problem is that it sucks out all the warm air from the workshop and increases our heating bills. One of the better solutions is a dust extraction unit, this recycles the air thus preserving the heat. When choosing a system you really need to know what you are looking for, because many systems masquerading under the name 'dust extractor' are really chip extractors. There is usually an expensive converter to make it in to a dust extractor which takes up almost as much space again. The difference between them is the rate at which the air passes through the filter bags. This needs to be slow if the fine dust particles are to be retained. While this option is probably the best for most small workshops, it starts to cost more than the lathe. Mine is a 2 hp system (chip extractor) with a long 4 in diameter hose to the lathe, I would have it nearer for greater efficiency, but the noise! One advantage is that they can be left running to clear the atmosphere while you take a break.

Safety is always a compromise on long term hazards between comfort of working, cost and introducing other hazards. Safety has to be considered as an integral part of the workshop and not an expensive luxury to be bought when times are good. It won't remove the legacy built up over the previous years. If you can't do it safely then don't do it.

WHERE TO FROM HERE

I would hope that at this stage you are completely competent with the process of turning, with all the tools, and with cutting the wood and are now ready to make your first project.

For most projects the turning is a small proportion of the total work involved, the actual sequence of events might look something like this:

1. Planning. The first and most important stage, this is the point at which all the decisions are made, from selecting the project to what you are going to do with it when it is finished. Get this part right and the rest will just fall into place.

   Having chosen a project and a suitable design the next critical part is selecting the tree or timber and marking it out ready for cutting. This is where much greater knowledge regarding the trees is essential, whether it is for structural or asthetic reasons or most likely a combination of both. We need to know which type of tree to use, how to cut it up, how it should be seasoned and how it reacts to being turned.

2. Execution. This should now be a matter of following through the process of preparing the wood for the lathe and completing the turning operation.

3. Finishing. One of the biggest problems with turning is that most turners want instant results with instant finishes. This very often dictates the method of finishing rather than the purpose of the object. Quick drying oils, waxes, and hard finishes can cause problems later on if they are inappropriate for the purpose of the finished object. Did you know that while some finishes will dry in a few minutes they can take up to a week to harden or cure. In the meantime you may be trying to polish a 'soft' surface. Compatability between finishes is also a problem.

This is just the start, make the most of it and enjoy your turning.

Reference

1) The action of cutting tools. Machinery's Yellowback Series No 31. The Machinery Publishing Co. Ltd.

INDEX

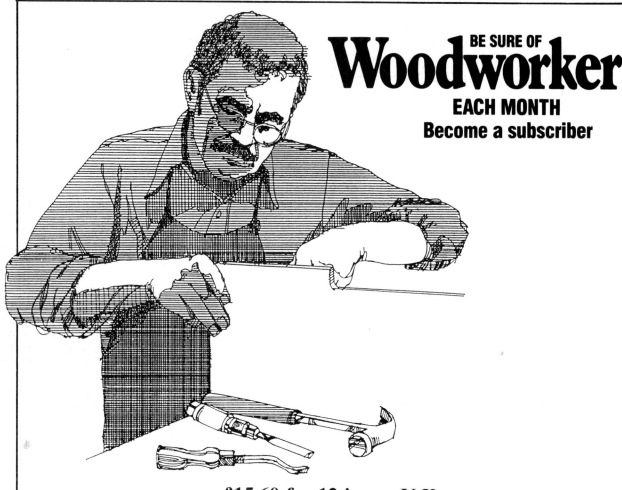